I0701255

BETWEEN INSTINCT AND REASON

THE ROLE OF FEAR IN HUMAN SURVIVAL

DAVID SANDUA

*"Fear is a natural reaction to the unknown;
learning to master it is essential for survival."*

Marie Curie

Index

I. Introduction

One of the most fundamental aspects of human behavior is the instinct of fear, a primal response deeply ingrained in our biology to protect us from harm. Throughout evolution, fear has played a crucial role in ensuring the survival of our species, alerting us to potential threats and triggering physiological responses to maximize our chances of escape or defense. However, as society has advanced and the dangers we face have evolved, the role of fear has become more complex. While fear remains a powerful force that can impede our ability to think and act rationally in stressful situations, it can also be managed and harnessed through reason and modern technology. This essay will explore the intricate balance between instinct and reason in the context of fear, examining how mastering this primal emotion is essential for human survival in an increasingly complex and unpredictable world.

Definition of fear and its evolutionary basis

The evolutionary basis of fear is deeply rooted in our biological mechanisms, serving as a critical survival tool that has been honed over millennia. Fear, defined as an intense emotional response triggered by a real or perceived threat, activates the body's fight-or-flight response, preparing us to either confront or flee from danger. This primal instinct is a remnant of our ancestors' need to avoid predators and other life-threatening situations, ensuring their survival in a hostile environment. While fear can sometimes be irrational or overwhelming, it is ultimately a necessary adaptation that has allowed humans to thrive and propagate. By understanding the evolutionary origins of fear, we can appreciate its role in keeping us safe and alert in a dangerous world. Through a combination of reason, resilience, and education, we can harness the power of fear to enhance our ability to navigate adversity and emerge stronger on the other side.

Overview of fear's role in human survival

In understanding fear's role in human survival, it is crucial to acknowledge that this innate emotion has been intricately woven into our evolutionary history as a means of protecting us from potential threats. From the primitive fight-or-flight response designed to increase our chances of survival in the face of danger to the complex interplay between fear and reason in modern society, fear serves as a powerful tool that can either hinder or enhance our ability to navigate challenging situations. By recognizing fear as a natural and adaptive response, individuals can begin to cultivate a greater sense of self-awareness and resilience, allowing them to confront and ultimately overcome their fears through deliberate practice and exposure. Through a combination of psychological techniques and practical exercises, individuals can learn to harness the power of fear, transforming it from a hindrance into a valuable ally in the pursuit of personal growth and well-being.

Thesis statement: Exploring the dual nature of fear as both a survival mechanism and a challenge to overcome through reason and training

In exploring the dual nature of fear as both a survival mechanism and a challenge to be overcome through reason and training, it becomes clear that fear is a fundamental aspect of human existence. It is undeniable that fear has played a crucial role in our evolutionary development, allowing our ancestors to recognize and respond to danger in order to ensure survival. However, as society has progressed and the threats we face have evolved, the need to control and master fear has become increasingly important. By harnessing the power of reason and implementing training techniques, individuals can learn to mitigate the impact of fear in high-stress situations. Through systematic desensitization and gradual exposure, individuals can confront and conquer their fears, ultimately enhancing their ability to remain calm and composed when faced with challenges. As we navigate the complexities of the modern world, understanding and managing fear is not only crucial for survival but also for personal growth and resilience in the face of adversity.

II. The Biological Basis of Fear

Throughout human evolution, fear has played a crucial role in ensuring our survival. Rooted in the biological makeup of our brains, fear serves as a mechanism to alert us to potential dangers and trigger a fight or flight response. This instinctual reaction is deeply ingrained in our DNA, dating back to our earliest ancestors who relied on fear to navigate through a hostile environment. However, as humanity has progressed and developed sophisticated cognitive abilities, we have also learned to temper and control our fear responses through reason and rationality. This delicate balance between instinct and intellect is what distinguishes us from other species, allowing us to assess risks, evaluate dangers, and make informed decisions in the face of adversity. By understanding the biological basis of fear, we can harness its power to sharpen our senses, sharpen our focus, and ultimately enhance our chances of survival in an ever-changing world.

Neurological pathways involved in fear response

When faced with a threatening situation, the brain quickly activates a series of neurological pathways involved in the fear response. The amygdala, a small almond-shaped structure deep within the brain, plays a central role in processing fear-related signals and coordinating the body's response to danger. As information about a potential threat is received, the amygdala sends out signals to release stress hormones like adrenaline, preparing the body for a fight-or-flight response. Additionally, the prefrontal cortex, known for its role in higher cognitive functions such as reasoning and decision-making, also interacts with the amygdala to help regulate fear responses. Research has shown that individuals who are better able to engage their prefrontal cortex during fear-inducing situations exhibit greater control over their emotional reactions. Understanding the intricate interplay between these brain regions sheds light on how fear can be modulated and managed through a combination of biological and cognitive processes, ultimately leading to more adaptive responses in the face of danger.

The fight or flight mechanism

In the realm of human survival, the fight or flight mechanism plays a crucial role in responding to threats and ensuring our safety. This innate response, deeply rooted in our evolutionary history, triggers a cascade of physiological changes that prepare us to confront or flee from potential dangers. While this instinctual reaction can be life-saving in certain situations, it is also important to recognize the limitations of this primal response. Modern society presents a myriad of complex challenges that cannot always be resolved through simple fight or flight reactions. As such, the ability to engage reason and rationality becomes paramount in navigating the complexities of our world. By harnessing our cognitive abilities, we can evaluate threats more effectively, devise strategic solutions, and ultimately transcend our instinctual responses to fear. In this way, the fight or flight mechanism is not a static force but rather a tool to be honed and integrated into our broader capacity for survival and adaptation.

Hormonal responses to perceived threats

In response to perceived threats, the human body undergoes intricate hormonal changes that have been shaped by millennia of evolution. When faced with danger, the brain signals the release of stress hormones like cortisol and adrenaline, preparing the body for fight or flight. These hormonal responses are essential in ensuring survival in life-threatening situations, as they increase heart rate, boost energy levels, and sharpen focus. However, in modern society, where threats are often more psychological than physical, these automatic responses can sometimes be detrimental. It is crucial for individuals to learn how to manage these hormonal reactions through rational thinking and mental fortitude. By cultivating awareness of one's own fear responses and developing techniques to regulate them, individuals can harness the power of fear without being overwhelmed by it. Through a combination of biological understanding and psychological strategies, humans can learn to navigate the delicate balance between instinctive fear and reasoned response, ultimately enhancing their ability to survive and thrive in an increasingly complex world.

III. Historical Perspectives on Fear and Survival

Throughout history, fear has played a pivotal role in the survival of the human species. From ancient times when early humans relied on fear to avoid predators and other dangers, to modern society where fear is still a potent tool in protecting oneself from harm, the evolution of this instinct has been a constant thread. Looking back, we can see how fear has shaped human behavior, driving us to seek safety and avoid threats. The historical perspectives on fear and survival provide valuable insights into how our ancestors navigated a hostile world, relying on their instincts to make split-second decisions that could mean life or death. By understanding how fear has been integral to our survival as a species, we can better appreciate its profound impact on our lives today. Fear, while often seen as a negative emotion, has served a critical purpose in keeping humans safe and ensuring our continued existence in a dangerous world.

Fear in prehistoric times

Throughout prehistoric times, fear played a critical role in the survival of early humans. In a world filled with predators and dangers at every turn, fear served as a powerful instinctual response that allowed our ancestors to react quickly and decisively to threats. These primitive fears were ingrained in the very fabric of our biology, guiding our actions and helping us navigate the treacherous landscape of the ancient world. In the face of predators like saber-toothed tigers and other formidable foes, fear kept our ancestors alert and ready to fight or flee at a moment's notice. Without this primal sense of fear, early humans would have struggled to survive in a hostile and unforgiving environment. As we reflect on the role of fear in prehistoric times, it becomes clear that this instinct was a vital tool that enabled our ancestors to navigate the dangers of their world and ultimately ensure their survival.

Evolution of fear responses from ancient to modern humans

Evolutionary studies have shown that fear responses have deep roots in the history of human survival, originating from our ancient ancestors who relied on these instincts to protect themselves from predators. Over time, as humans evolved and developed more complex societies, the nature of fear responses has also evolved. While ancient humans relied primarily on fight or flight responses to threats, modern humans have developed more nuanced and varied fear responses. Today, fear manifests in ways that are not always directly related to physical danger but can also be triggered by societal pressures, psychological stressors, and existential threats. The evolution of fear responses from ancient to modern humans highlights the adaptive nature of this primal instinct, showing how it continues to play a crucial role in our survival and decision-making processes. By understanding the evolution of fear responses, we can better navigate the complex world we live in and develop strategies to manage and overcome our fears effectively.

Comparative analysis of fear in humans and other animals

Throughout the evolution of life on Earth, fear has been a fundamental survival mechanism for both humans and other animals. Research has shown that the response to fear is deeply rooted in our brain structures and hormonal systems, indicating a commonality in the experience of fear across species. This comparative analysis allows us to understand fear as a universal response to perceived threats, triggering the fight-or-flight response in all living beings. While humans possess the unique ability to rationalize and regulate their fear response through cognitive processes, the underlying physiological mechanisms remain similar across species. By acknowledging the similarities in how fear operates in humans and other animals, we can gain a deeper understanding of its role in shaping behavior and ensuring survival. This comparative perspective underscores the importance of respecting the primal nature of fear while also harnessing our cognitive abilities to effectively manage and overcome it.

IV. Fear as a Survival Mechanism

Fear, deeply rooted in our evolutionary past, serves as a fundamental survival mechanism crucial for our existence. This primal instinct, often triggered in response to potential threats, allows us to react swiftly to dangerous situations and avoid harm. However, while fear is a necessary tool for survival, individuals must also learn to harness and control it effectively. Through training and practice, individuals such as firefighters and soldiers demonstrate the ability to manage fear in high-stress environments, enabling them to perform optimally under pressure. By applying psychological and physical techniques, individuals can improve their capacity to remain composed and rational in the face of fear. Confronting fears head-on, utilizing strategies like gradual exposure and systematic desensitization, can empower individuals to overcome a wide range of phobias and anxieties. Ultimately, mastering fear not only enhances physical survival but also enhances overall quality of life by fostering resilience and self-awareness. Through understanding and managing fear, individuals can transform it from a potential adversary into an invaluable ally.

Protective role of fear in avoiding danger

Throughout history, fear has played a crucial role in ensuring human survival by prompting us to avoid potential dangers. When faced with a threat, our bodies respond instinctively, releasing adrenaline and preparing us for fight or flight. This automatic reaction has been vital in helping our ancestors escape predators and other life-threatening situations. In modern times, fear continues to serve as a protective mechanism, alerting us to potential risks and prompting us to take necessary precautions. However, it is essential to recognize that while fear can be a powerful motivator, it can also be overwhelming and debilitating if not managed effectively. By understanding the triggers of fear and learning to control our responses through rational thinking and preparation, we can harness the protective role of fear while still maintaining composure and making informed decisions in the face of danger. Ultimately, mastering fear allows us to navigate high-risk situations with confidence and resilience, enhancing our chances of survival and overall well-being.

Fear-induced heightened awareness

In addition to the physiological responses that fear triggers, it also plays a significant role in enhancing our awareness of potential threats in our environment. Studies have shown that fear-induced heightened awareness can improve our ability to detect and respond to dangers more quickly and effectively. This heightened state of alertness is a result of the release of stress hormones, such as adrenaline, which sharpen our focus and increase our sensitivity to stimuli. By being more attuned to our surroundings when experiencing fear, we are better equipped to assess risks and make split-second decisions in challenging situations. Furthermore, this heightened awareness can be honed and refined through training and practice, allowing individuals to harness the positive aspects of fear while minimizing its negative impact on performance. Ultimately, understanding and mastering fear-induced heightened awareness can be a valuable tool for enhancing human survival and wellbeing in a variety of contexts.

Case studies of fear contributing to survival in extreme conditions

Furthermore, case studies of fear contributing to survival in extreme conditions provide valuable insights into how fear can be a powerful motivator in life-threatening situations. For example, studies of individuals who have survived natural disasters or extreme wilderness conditions often highlight the role fear played in their ability to make quick decisions and take necessary actions to ensure their survival. In these cases, fear acts as a catalyst for heightened awareness and increased adrenaline, allowing individuals to tap into their primal instincts and mobilize their resources effectively. By examining these real-life scenarios, we can better understand the adaptive nature of fear and its potential to drive individuals to push beyond their perceived limits. These case studies serve as compelling evidence that fear, when harnessed and channeled effectively, can be a key factor in overcoming extreme challenges and emerging victorious in the face of adversity.

V. The Psychology of Fear

In exploring the psychology of fear, it becomes evident that this innate emotion has played a crucial role in human survival throughout history. As our ancestors faced predators and other threats in their environment, fear served as a powerful survival mechanism, triggering the fight-or-flight response that ensured their immediate safety. However, in the modern world, where many of these physical dangers have been reduced, fear continues to manifest in more complex and nuanced ways. Understanding the mechanisms of fear in the human brain can empower individuals to navigate high-stress situations with greater resilience and control. By recognizing the triggers of fear and implementing strategies to manage this powerful emotion, individuals can harness fear as a source of motivation and self-awareness, rather than allowing it to paralyze or overwhelm them. Through a combination of psychological techniques and rational thought, individuals can cultivate a sense of calm and perspective that enables them to confront their fears head-on, ultimately leading to personal growth and increased emotional resilience. Thus, by acknowledging and mastering the psychology of fear, individuals can transform this primal instinct into a tool for self-improvement and adaptive survival in the modern world.

Cognitive aspects of fear processing

Furthermore, the cognitive aspects of fear processing shed light on the intricate mechanisms that govern our reactions to perceived threats. Studies show that the amygdala plays a crucial role in processing fear, triggering a cascade of physiological responses aimed at preparing the body for fight or flight. However, recent research suggests that cognitive appraisal plays a significant role in modulating our fear response. By interpreting and evaluating the perceived threat, individuals can influence the intensity and duration of their fear response. This highlights the importance of cognitive-behavioral techniques in managing fear, such as mindfulness and positive reframing. By harnessing the power of reasoning and self-awareness, individuals can reframe their perceptions of fear-inducing situations, leading to more adaptive and controlled responses. Ultimately, understanding the cognitive underpinnings of fear processing provides a pathway towards mastery over this primal instinct, empowering individuals to navigate challenging situations with resilience and composure.

Emotional and psychological impacts of fear

Throughout history, fear has played a crucial role in human survival, triggering our fight or flight response when faced with danger. However, the emotional and psychological impact of fear goes beyond immediate physical reactions. Fear can lead to chronic stress, anxiety disorders, and other mental health issues if not properly managed. Understanding the root causes of our fears and learning to confront and conquer them is essential for maintaining mental well-being. Conquering fear involves a combination of cognitive strategies, such as reframing negative thoughts, and behavioral techniques, like exposure therapy. By gradually facing our fears and learning to reframe our perspective, we can reduce the emotional toll of fear and build resilience in the face of adversity. Ultimately, by mastering our fears, we can not only enhance our quality of life but also strengthen our overall mental health and emotional well-being.

Fear's effect on decision-making processes

In the realm of decision-making processes, fear plays a significant role in shaping our choices and actions. When faced with a threatening situation, fear triggers a primal response that can influence our cognitive processes and judgment. This is because fear activates the amygdala, the part of the brain responsible for processing emotions and storing memories related to fear-inducing stimuli. As a result, individuals experiencing fear may prioritize immediate safety over long-term consequences, leading to impulsive decisions based on survival instincts rather than rational thinking. Moreover, heightened levels of fear can impair cognitive functions such as problem-solving and critical thinking, making it difficult to make strategic decisions in high-pressure situations. Therefore, understanding the impact of fear on decision-making processes is crucial in developing effective strategies to manage and mitigate its effects, ultimately leading to more rational and calculated choices even in the face of fear-inducing circumstances.

VI. Fear in Children and Development

Furthermore, the impact of fear on children's development cannot be understated. Research has shown that fear in early childhood can have long-lasting effects on cognitive and emotional development. Children who are exposed to chronic or extreme fear may struggle with impulse control, have difficulty forming secure attachments, and exhibit symptoms of anxiety and depression later in life. This underscores the importance of providing a safe and nurturing environment for children to grow and thrive. By understanding how fear can shape a child's development, parents, caregivers, and educators can implement strategies to help children cope with and overcome their fears in a healthy way. Encouraging open communication, providing reassurance, and teaching coping mechanisms are just some of the ways in which adults can support children in navigating their fears and promoting resilience. Ultimately, recognizing and addressing fear in children is crucial for fostering their emotional well-being and overall development.

Developmental stages of fear

Moreover, understanding the developmental stages of fear is crucial in mastering this primal instinct. From infancy, humans exhibit a rudimentary form of fear, such as the fear of loud noises or sudden movements. As individuals grow, they undergo various stages where fears become more complex and nuanced, influenced by both innate biological responses and learned experiences. These developmental stages shape how individuals perceive and respond to threats, impacting their ability to manage fear effectively. By examining these stages, individuals can identify the root causes of their fears and develop strategies to address them. This deeper understanding of the progression of fear allows individuals to confront and overcome their fears in a systematic manner, leading to greater emotional resilience and self-mastery. Ultimately, mastering fear at each stage of development is essential for achieving a balanced and empowered approach to survival in the face of danger.

Learning from fearful experiences

In the realm of human survival, the ability to learn from fearful experiences is a crucial skill that can mean the difference between life and death. Overcoming fear requires a combination of instinctual responses and rational thought processes, allowing individuals to navigate dangerous situations with a clear mind and effective strategy. By acknowledging fear as a natural response to threats, individuals can begin to understand and control their reactions, ultimately leading to improved decision-making and survival outcomes. Through training and practice, individuals can develop the necessary skills to manage fear in high-stress environments, enabling them to perform at their best even in the face of adversity. By confronting fears head-on, individuals can gradually desensitize themselves to these threats, ultimately empowering themselves to overcome challenges and achieve success. This process not only enhances physical survival but also fosters a deeper sense of self-awareness and resilience, ultimately leading to a more fulfilling and enriched life. Thus, learning from fearful experiences is not only essential for survival but also for personal growth and development.

Teaching children to manage fear

In the modern world, teaching children to manage fear is a crucial skill for their emotional development and overall well-being. By equipping young individuals with strategies to navigate and regulate their fears, we empower them to face challenges confidently and make sound decisions under pressure. One approach to teaching children to manage fear is through mindfulness techniques, which encourage them to acknowledge their emotions without judgment and cultivate a sense of inner calm. Additionally, exposure therapy can be utilized to gradually desensitize children to specific fears, helping them build resilience and confidence over time. By incorporating these tools into a child's education and upbringing, we can instill in them the ability to confront and overcome fears proactively, ultimately fostering a sense of self-assurance and adaptability in the face of adversity. With proper guidance and support, children can learn to navigate the complex terrain of fear, emerging stronger and more resilient individuals in the process.

VII. Fear in the Modern World

In contemporary society, fear manifests in multifaceted ways, influenced by technological advancements, globalization, and the media. The hyperconnectivity of the modern world exposes individuals to a constant stream of information, often highlighting threats and dangers from all corners of the globe. This inundation of potentially fear-inducing stimuli can overwhelm the psyche, leading to heightened levels of anxiety and stress. Moreover, the rapid pace of technological innovation has introduced new sources of fear, such as privacy breaches, cyber-attacks, and the ethical implications of artificial intelligence. In this context, it becomes essential for individuals to cultivate a nuanced understanding of fear and develop strategies to navigate through the complexities of the contemporary landscape. By harnessing the power of reason, critical thinking, and emotional intelligence, individuals can effectively manage fear, discerning between genuine threats and perceived dangers, ultimately empowering themselves to thrive in the face of adversity.

Rational versus irrational fears

In the realm of fears that humans experience, there exists a dichotomy between rational and irrational fears. Rational fears are grounded in real and objective threats that pose a genuine danger to survival. These fears serve a crucial evolutionary purpose, as they compel individuals to take necessary precautions and avoid harm. On the other hand, irrational fears are not based on verifiable threats but are often products of imagination or past traumas. While rational fears can be rationalized and managed through reason, irrational fears tend to be more challenging to overcome due to their elusive nature. Understanding the distinction between these two types of fears is essential in developing effective strategies for coping with them. By acknowledging the source of one's fears and evaluating their validity, individuals can work towards mastering their emotions and cultivating a sense of inner peace and security in the face of adversity.

Fear induced by modern societal factors

Through the lens of modern societal factors, fear takes on new dimensions, often induced by a plethora of stimuli that our ancestors did not have to contend with. The constant bombardment of information through social media, news outlets, and advertising can trigger heightened levels of anxiety and fear in individuals, leading to a sense of overwhelm and helplessness. This influx of information, coupled with the pressure to conform to societal standards and expectations, can create a breeding ground for fear to thrive. Moreover, the fast-paced nature of modern life, filled with uncertainty and unpredictability, can exacerbate feelings of fear and insecurity. As we navigate this complex landscape, it becomes crucial to recognize the sources of our fears, analyze them critically, and develop strategies to confront and overcome them. By understanding the root causes of fear induced by modern societal factors, individuals can empower themselves to navigate the challenges of contemporary life with greater resilience and mental fortitude.

The impact of media on fear perception

The influence of media on fear perception cannot be understated in today's society. The proliferation of sensationalized news stories, violent images, and fear-inducing narratives through various platforms has contributed to an increase in fear and anxiety among the population. Studies have shown that constant exposure to negative news can heighten feelings of vulnerability and insecurity, leading individuals to perceive the world as more dangerous than it actually is. This distorted perception not only affects people's mental well-being but also their decision-making processes and behavior. Media plays a significant role in shaping our understanding of risk and danger, often emphasizing rare and extreme events that evoke strong emotional responses. As such, it is crucial for individuals to critically evaluate the information they consume and strive to balance exposure to fearful content with more positive and factual sources. By becoming more discerning consumers of media, we can mitigate the impact of sensationalism on our fear perception and cultivate a more rational and resilient mindset.

VIII. Fear and Culture

When considering the interplay between fear and culture, it is evident that these two aspects of human existence are deeply intertwined. Culture plays a significant role in shaping our fears, as societal norms, beliefs, and values can influence what we perceive as threatening or dangerous. For example, certain cultures may instill a fear of failure or shame, leading individuals to avoid taking risks or pursuing their goals. On the other hand, cultures that prioritize bravery and resilience may help individuals confront their fears head-on and develop a sense of courage. Moreover, fear can also shape culture, as collective fears often inform societal structures and behaviors. Whether it is a fear of other cultures, a fear of change, or a fear of the unknown, these shared fears can impact how communities interact and make decisions. In essence, fear and culture are inextricably linked, influencing each other in a complex dance that ultimately shapes human behavior and society as a whole.

Cultural variations in fear responses

Throughout history, human fear responses have been shaped by cultural variations, reflecting the unique beliefs, norms, and values of different societies. For example, in collectivist cultures where group harmony is paramount, fear may be suppressed or masked to avoid disrupting social cohesion. On the other hand, individualistic cultures may encourage more open expressions of fear as a sign of vulnerability or authenticity. These cultural differences not only influence how fear is perceived and experienced but also impact how individuals are expected to respond to fear in various contexts. In some cultures, fear may be seen as a weakness to be overcome through courage and resilience, while in others, it may be embraced as a natural part of life to be accepted and managed. Understanding these cultural variations in fear responses is crucial for developing strategies to effectively address and mitigate fear in diverse populations, ultimately contributing to a more holistic approach to promoting mental health and well-being across different cultural contexts.

Fear in folklore and mythology

Throughout folklore and mythology, fear has often been depicted as a powerful force that can both protect and harm individuals. In these narratives, fear is not simply an emotion but a supernatural entity that can shape destinies and influence behaviors. From the Greek myth of Medusa turning men to stone with her terrifying gaze to the Grim Reaper embodying the ultimate fear of death, these stories reflect how fear has been woven into the fabric of human consciousness for centuries. Fear in folklore serves as a cautionary tale, warning individuals of the consequences of recklessness and hubris. It reminds us of our vulnerability and the need to respect the unknown forces that govern our lives. By exploring these tales, we can gain a deeper understanding of the role fear plays in shaping human behavior and attitudes towards the unpredictable and the supernatural. Through these stories, we can see fear not just as a primal instinct for survival, but as a complex and multifaceted phenomenon that can both paralyze and empower us.

Fear's role in cultural rituals and traditions

Throughout various cultural rituals and traditions, fear plays a significant role in shaping the beliefs and practices of a community. From initiation ceremonies to harvest festivals, fear is often used as a tool to evoke emotions, create bonds among participants, and reinforce social norms. In many cultures, rituals involving fear are believed to bring communities together, instilling a sense of unity and shared experience. The fear experienced during these rituals can also serve as a form of catharsis, allowing individuals to confront their anxieties in a controlled setting. By facing their fears within the context of a ritual, participants can gain a sense of empowerment and resilience, ultimately leading to personal growth and transformation. In this way, fear in cultural rituals and traditions acts as a mechanism for fostering social cohesion, personal development, and a connection to the collective identity of a community.

IX. Fear and Religion

In exploring the intricate relationship between fear and religion, it becomes apparent that these two powerful forces have intersected and influenced each other throughout history. Religion often serves as a source of solace in times of fear and uncertainty, providing believers with a sense of comfort and security. The belief in a higher power can help individuals navigate frightening situations and find strength in their faith. Conversely, fear can also be a driving force behind religious practices, as the fear of divine punishment or the unknown can shape people's beliefs and behaviors. This dynamic interplay between fear and religion highlights the complex ways in which human psychology and spirituality intertwine. By examining how fear and religion interact, we can gain a deeper understanding of the intricate mechanisms that guide human behavior and belief systems. Ultimately, this exploration sheds light on the power of both fear and religion in shaping individual and collective experiences.

Fear in religious teachings and texts

Throughout religious teachings and texts, fear plays a prominent role in shaping beliefs and behaviors. From the fear of divine punishment for sinful actions to the fear of a higher power's judgment after death, fear is often used as a tool to enforce moral codes and guide followers towards obedience. This fear can create a sense of control and discipline within religious communities, acting as a deterrent against wrongdoing and a motivator for righteous living. However, some argue that this fear-based approach can also lead to feelings of guilt, shame, and anxiety, ultimately impacting an individual's mental well-being. It is essential to examine the balance between instilling a healthy reverence and respect for the divine and avoiding instilling a paralyzing fear that stifles personal growth and autonomy. By critically analyzing the role of fear in religious teachings, we can better understand its impact on individuals and society as a whole.

The use of fear as a tool for moral guidance

In considering the use of fear as a tool for moral guidance, it becomes apparent that while fear can be a powerful motivator for shaping behavior, its effectiveness is limited in the long run. Fear may lead individuals to comply with moral standards out of a sense of self-preservation, but this compliance is often superficial and does not address the underlying values and principles that should guide ethical decision-making. Moreover, relying solely on fear to dictate moral behavior can lead to negative consequences, such as increased anxiety, paranoia, and a lack of genuine empathy towards others. Instead, a more sustainable approach to moral guidance involves cultivating a deep understanding of one's values and beliefs, and using reason and compassion to navigate ethical dilemmas. By fostering a sense of intrinsic motivation and moral integrity, individuals can make decisions that are not only in line with societal norms but also reflect a genuine commitment to doing what is right, even in the absence of external threats or punishments.

Fear and religious rituals

In the realm of religious rituals, fear plays a distinctive role in guiding devotees towards a deeper connection with the divine. Many religious practices incorporate elements of fear, whether through awe-inspiring ceremonies, rituals of purification, or teachings on morality and consequences. Fear, in this context, can serve as a motivator for individuals to adhere to religious teachings and uphold moral standards out of reverence for a higher power or fear of divine retribution. Additionally, the fear of the unknown and the mysteries of the spiritual realm can inspire awe and humility in the face of the divine, leading to a profound sense of reverence and submission. In essence, fear in religious rituals can serve as a powerful tool for shaping beliefs, behaviors, and attitudes, ultimately contributing to the spiritual growth and development of individuals within a religious community.

X. Fear in Literature and Art

Fear in literature and art has long been utilized as a powerful tool to evoke emotional responses and to explore the depths of the human psyche. Authors and artists have skillfully woven themes of fear into their works, creating compelling narratives that resonate with audiences on a profound level. Fear in literature often serves as a vehicle for exploring existential questions, societal anxieties, and personal demons. Characters face their fears head-on, forcing readers to confront their own fears and vulnerabilities. Similarly, in art, fear can be depicted through imagery that is both unsettling and thought-provoking, challenging viewers to confront their deepest fears and emotions. By tapping into universal fears like death, loss, and the unknown, literature and art have the ability to connect people through shared experiences of fear and vulnerability. Through the examination of fear in literature and art, we gain valuable insights into the human condition and the complexities of our emotional landscape.

Representation of fear in classical literature

Furthermore, fear's representation in classical literature provides rich insights into the complexities of human emotion and behavior. In works like Homer's "The Iliad" or Dante's "Inferno," fear is often depicted as a powerful force that can drive individuals to both heroic feats and tragic mistakes. These narratives demonstrate how fear can consume characters, leading them to act irrationally or courageously in the face of adversity. Through the lens of classical literature, we can see how fear has been a timeless theme that resonates with readers across diverse cultures and time periods. By examining how fear is portrayed in these texts, we gain a deeper understanding of its role in shaping human experiences and decisions. Ultimately, classical literature offers us a nuanced and multifaceted perspective on fear, highlighting its complex interplay with courage, morality, and fate.

Fear as a theme in modern literature

Fear, as a prevalent theme in modern literature, serves as a powerful tool for exploring the complexities of the human experience. Writers often utilize fear to delve into the depths of human emotions, motivations, and vulnerabilities. Through the depiction of characters grappling with fear, authors can touch on universal truths about the human condition while also shedding light on societal issues and cultural anxieties. In modern literature, fear is not merely a plot device but rather a lens through which deeper themes are explored, such as identity, power dynamics, and moral dilemmas. By examining fear in various contexts and manifestations, writers can provide valuable insights into the human psyche and the ways in which individuals navigate the challenges of existence. Furthermore, fear in modern literature often serves as a mirror reflecting the anxieties and uncertainties of contemporary society, inviting readers to confront their own fears and anxieties in a cathartic and illuminating way.

Exploration of fear in visual arts

In visual arts, the exploration of fear is a multifaceted and complex endeavor that delves into the depths of human emotions and psyche. Artists have long utilized various mediums such as painting, sculpture, and photography to evoke feelings of fear in their audience, often challenging societal norms and conventions. Through the use of symbolism, color, and composition, artists are able to create powerful and evocative pieces that tap into our deepest fears and anxieties. The representation of fear in art allows viewers to confront their own emotions and fears in a safe and controlled environment, fostering introspection and self-awareness. By confronting our fears through visual art, we are able to navigate the complexities of our own emotions and better understand the human experience as a whole. This exploration of fear in visual arts not only serves as a form of catharsis for both the artist and the viewer but also as a means of connecting with our shared humanity and understanding the universal nature of fear.

XI. Fear and Philosophy

In examining the intersection of fear and philosophy, one cannot overlook the intrinsic connection between our primal instincts and higher cognitive functions. Fear, as a natural response designed to safeguard our survival, has been integral to our existence since the earliest days of humanity. However, the evolution of our understanding and perception of fear has revealed that it can be both a hindrance and a catalyst for growth. Through the lens of philosophy, the discourse on fear delves into the intricate balance between instinctual reactions and rational thought, emphasizing the importance of mastering our fears through introspection and intellectual engagement. By exploring the complexities of fear through a philosophical framework, we can begin to unravel the mysteries of this powerful emotion and harness its potential for personal development and resilience in the face of adversity. Fear, when properly understood and navigated, can serve as a gateway to deeper self-awareness and profound philosophical insights.

Philosophical interpretations of fear

In exploring the philosophical interpretations of fear, it becomes evident that this primal emotion serves as a powerful force that shapes our actions and decisions. Fear, often associated with vulnerability and uncertainty, has been a subject of contemplation for philosophers throughout history. Some view fear as a necessary component of human existence, driving individuals to seek protection and security in a hostile world. Others see fear as a hindrance to personal growth and enlightenment, preventing individuals from fully embracing life and its challenges. However, it is essential to recognize that fear, when understood and managed effectively, can be a valuable tool for self-discovery and transformation. By delving into the depths of our fears, we can uncover hidden truths about ourselves and confront our insecurities head-on, ultimately leading to personal growth and resilience. Thus, philosophical interpretations of fear offer a nuanced perspective on this complex emotion, shedding light on its potential as both a hindrance and a catalyst for self-improvement.

Fear and existentialism

Moreover, existentialism offers a unique perspective on fear, suggesting that it is not just a biological response but a fundamental aspect of human existence. Existentialist philosophers like Kierkegaard and Nietzsche argue that fear is intricately tied to the human experience of confronting the unknown and the uncertainties of life. In this view, fear is not just a primitive survival mechanism but a deep-seated emotion that arises from our awareness of our own mortality and the inherent meaninglessness of the universe. By embracing the existentialist perspective on fear, individuals can move beyond simply managing or overcoming their fears to truly understanding and accepting them as an essential part of the human condition. This approach allows for a more profound exploration of the role of fear in shaping our beliefs, values, and ultimately, our understanding of ourselves and the world around us. Through the lens of existentialism, fear becomes not just a hindrance to be overcome, but a powerful force that can drive personal growth and self-discovery.

The role of fear in ethical decision-making

Throughout human history, fear has played a critical role in ethical decision-making, acting as a powerful motivator that pushes individuals to consider the consequences of their actions. When faced with situations that challenge their moral compass, fear can serve as a moral compass itself, guiding individuals towards decisions that align with their values and principles. In this way, fear can act as a safeguard against unethical behavior, prompting individuals to pause and reflect on the potential impact of their choices. However, fear can also be a double-edged sword, leading individuals to make hasty decisions out of panic or self-preservation. It is essential, therefore, to strike a balance between acknowledging and respecting fear as a valuable emotional response while also recognizing its limitations in guiding ethical decision-making. By understanding the role of fear in ethical dilemmas, individuals can navigate complex situations with greater clarity and integrity.

XII. Fear and Science

Throughout history, fear has been a powerful force guiding human behavior and decision-making. As a primal instinct, fear has played a crucial role in ensuring our survival by alerting us to potential dangers and triggering a fight-or-flight response. In the context of science, fear can motivate individuals to seek knowledge and understanding to mitigate perceived threats. However, the relationship between fear and science is intricate and multifaceted. While fear can drive scientific inquiry, it can also hinder progress by fostering reluctance to explore the unknown or challenging established beliefs. Thus, it is essential to strike a balance between acknowledging the role of fear in shaping our perceptions and leveraging the power of reason and evidence-based thinking to navigate uncertainties. By recognizing and managing our fears through the lens of scientific inquiry, we can harness their beneficial aspects while minimizing their disruptive influence on our pursuit of knowledge and progress.

Scientific understanding of fear

The scientific understanding of fear delves into the intricate mechanisms of the human brain and body when faced with a threat. Fear, as a primal instinct, triggers a cascade of reactions that prepare the individual for fight or flight, protecting them from harm. Through neuroscientific research, we now know that the amygdala plays a central role in processing fear responses, while the prefrontal cortex is involved in regulating and interpreting these signals. Understanding the biological basis of fear not only sheds light on its evolutionary purpose but also provides insights into how fear can be controlled and managed. By integrating knowledge from psychology, biology, and neuroscience, we can harness the power of reason to override instinctual fear responses, enabling individuals to confront their fears and thrive in challenging situations. This multidisciplinary approach offers a comprehensive understanding of fear, empowering individuals to navigate through life's uncertainties with resilience and courage.

Fear in scientific experimentation

Through the lens of scientific experimentation, fear becomes a critical factor that cannot be overlooked. The fear of the unknown, the fear of failure, and the fear of the potential consequences of groundbreaking discoveries all play a significant role in shaping the trajectory of research and innovation. It is imperative for scientists to acknowledge and address these fears, as they can either hinder or drive progress. Fear can lead to caution, ensuring thoroughness and precision in methodology, but it can also breed hesitancy and reluctance to take risks. In the realm of scientific experimentation, fear must be carefully navigated, balanced with rationality and objectivity. By understanding and harnessing fear, scientists can propel themselves towards new discoveries while mitigating potential risks. Ultimately, fear in scientific experimentation is a double-edged sword that must be wielded with caution and respect for its power to both hinder and drive progress in the pursuit of knowledge and innovation.

Fear's influence on scientific discovery

Furthermore, fear's influence on scientific discovery can be seen in the role it plays in motivating researchers to explore the unknown and push the boundaries of knowledge. The fear of the consequences of ignorance or the fear of failure can drive scientists to pursue innovative solutions to complex problems. This fear can spark creativity and inspire groundbreaking discoveries that have the potential to change the course of history. In the face of uncertainty and the unknown, fear can compel scientists to ask critical questions, challenge assumptions, and think outside the box. Without fear driving their curiosity and determination, many scientific breakthroughs may never have been achieved. Therefore, fear should be embraced as a powerful force that drives scientific progress and motivates researchers to explore new frontiers in search of truth and understanding. By harnessing fear's influence in a positive way, scientists can unlock new insights and make remarkable advancements in their fields.

XIII. Fear and Technology

In the modern age, fear and technology have become intertwined in complex ways that both heighten and mitigate our innate fears. While technology has provided numerous benefits and advancements that make our lives easier and safer, it has also introduced new sources of fear and anxiety. The rapid pace of technological innovation can lead to feelings of overwhelm and uncertainty, as individuals struggle to keep pace with the constant changes and developments in the digital landscape. Additionally, the rise of social media and interconnectedness has created a platform for the rapid spread of misinformation and fear-mongering, further exacerbating feelings of insecurity and mistrust. However, technology also offers tools and resources to help individuals manage and overcome their fears. Through virtual reality exposure therapy, biofeedback devices, and mindfulness apps, individuals can learn to confront and cope with their fears in a controlled and supportive environment. By harnessing the power of technology in this way, individuals can develop the skills and resilience needed to navigate an increasingly complex and uncertain world.

Technology-induced fears

Fear, a primal instinct deeply rooted in our evolutionary history, serves as a crucial mechanism for human survival. However, advancements in technology have introduced a new dimension to our fears, triggering concerns about privacy invasion, job displacement, and even existential threats from artificial intelligence. While these fears may seem valid in a rapidly changing world, it is essential to remember that fear, in its essence, is a tool designed to protect us. By harnessing rationality and critical thinking, we can navigate through these technological uncertainties with a composed and strategic mindset. Rather than succumbing to irrational dread, we must view technology-induced fears as challenges to be understood and overcome. Through education, adaptation, and collaboration, we can transform these fears into opportunities for growth and innovation, ultimately empowering ourselves to thrive in the face of technological advancements.

Technology as a tool to manage fear

In the modern age, technology serves as a powerful tool to manage and overcome fear. Advancements in virtual reality have provided a platform for exposure therapy, allowing individuals to confront their fears in a controlled environment. By simulating anxiety-inducing scenarios, individuals can gradually desensitize themselves to fear triggers, ultimately diminishing their impact in real-life situations. Moreover, wearable technology such as heart rate monitors and biofeedback devices offer real-time physiological data that can help individuals regulate their responses to fear. These tools enable users to identify signs of escalating anxiety and implement techniques to remain calm and composed. In essence, technology acts as a bridge between instinctual fear responses and rational control, offering innovative solutions for individuals to confront and manage their fears effectively. Through the integration of technology into fear management strategies, individuals can harness the power of reason to navigate threatening situations with clarity and resilience.

Future technologies addressing fear

It is evident that technology plays a crucial role in addressing fear, especially in the context of future advancements. One promising avenue for helping individuals confront their fears is the development of virtual reality (VR) technologies. By immersing users in simulated environments that trigger their fears in a controlled setting, VR can provide a safe space for exposure therapy. This approach can be particularly effective for phobias, PTSD, and anxiety disorders, allowing individuals to gradually confront and overcome their fears. Additionally, biofeedback devices that monitor physiological responses such as heart rate and breathing patterns can help individuals regulate their emotional states in real-time, enabling them to better manage fear and anxiety. As technology continues to evolve, we can expect even more innovative tools and methods to be developed, offering new ways to support individuals in facing and conquering their fears. Ultimately, future technologies have the potential to revolutionize the way we approach fear, empowering individuals to take control of their emotional responses and enhance their overall well-being.

XIV. Fear in the Media

Throughout history, fear has been utilized as a powerful tool in the media to evoke emotional responses and shape public opinion. The media has the ability to amplify fear by sensationalizing events and perpetuating a culture of anxiety. News outlets often focus on negative and fear-inducing stories to attract viewership, leading to a constant barrage of alarming headlines and images. This constant exposure to fear-inducing content can have a detrimental impact on individuals, increasing stress levels and contributing to feelings of helplessness and despair. Moreover, the media's portrayal of certain groups or events can exacerbate societal fears and perpetuate stereotypes, leading to prejudice and discrimination. In the age of social media, fear can spread rapidly, fuelling panic and misinformation. It is crucial for media outlets to exercise responsibility and balance in their reporting, ensuring that fear is not exploited for ratings or political gain. The media holds a significant influence over public perceptions and attitudes, making it imperative for journalists and media organizations to uphold ethical standards and strive for accuracy and balance in their reporting. By acknowledging the power of fear in the media and promoting responsible journalism, we can work towards a more informed and empowered society.

Media portrayal of fear

As fear is portrayed in the media, there is a tendency to sensationalize and exaggerate potential threats, shaping public perceptions and responses to various dangers. The media often focuses on worst-case scenarios, triggering a primal fear response in individuals that can lead to irrational behavior and anxiety. This constant bombardment of fear-inducing content can have detrimental effects on mental health, heightening stress levels and contributing to a culture of fear and paranoia. However, by critically analyzing media portrayals of fear and developing a sense of media literacy, individuals can learn to distinguish between legitimate concerns and exaggerated threats. Through education and awareness, people can cultivate a more rational and balanced approach to fear, helping to reduce the impact of sensationalized media on collective psyche. By understanding the power of media in shaping perceptions of fear, individuals can take steps to mitigate its influence and cultivate a more informed and resilient response to potential threats.

The role of news in spreading fear

In the realm of news media, there exists a delicate balance between informing the public and instilling fear. The role of news in spreading fear cannot be understated, as sensationalized headlines and constant updates on potential threats can exacerbate anxiety and contribute to a culture of fear. This fear-mongering approach may garner higher viewership and engagement, but it comes at the cost of fueling paranoia and mistrust. By sensationalizing certain events or amplifying the risks associated with particular issues, news outlets can create a distorted perception of reality that skews our understanding of the world around us. This cycle of fear perpetuation can have detrimental effects on individuals and society as a whole, leading to increased stress, anxiety, and divisiveness. It is crucial for news organizations to reflect on the ethical implications of their reporting and strive to provide balanced and accurate information that empowers the public rather than inciting panic. Only through responsible and thoughtful journalism can the media fulfill its duty to inform without spreading unnecessary fear.

Media literacy and fear management

Throughout history, media literacy has played an instrumental role in shaping public perceptions of fear. The rapid spread of information through various media platforms can often lead to the amplification of fear, as sensationalized headlines and images can trigger primal instincts of fight or flight. However, by cultivating media literacy skills, individuals can better discern fact from fiction, critically analyze sources, and navigate through the barrage of fear-inducing content. This ability to filter information allows for a more rational and measured response to threats, mitigating the overwhelming sense of fear that can arise from sensationalized news. Moreover, media literacy empowers individuals to confront fear-inducing narratives with a sense of agency and control, rather than succumbing to irrational panic. By mastering media literacy, people can effectively manage their fears and cultivate a more balanced and informed perspective on the world around them.

XV. Fear and Politics

While fear is often seen as a hindrance in political discourse, it can also serve as a powerful tool in shaping public opinion and driving societal change. Politicians have long understood the potency of fear in galvanizing support for their agendas, whether through exploiting existing fears or instigating new ones. From national security threats to economic uncertainty, fear has been used to sway public opinion and justify policies that may not align with the greater good. In this way, fear and politics have become intricately intertwined, with fear often being leveraged as a means of control and manipulation. However, it is crucial to recognize the dangers of allowing fear to dictate political decision-making, as it can lead to the erosion of civil liberties and the exacerbation of social divisions. By understanding the complex interplay between fear and politics, individuals can better navigate the political landscape and advocate for policies rooted in reason and compassion rather than fear-mongering tactics.

Use of fear in political discourse

Fear has long been a potent tool in political discourse, utilized by leaders to shape public perception and drive action. From ancient times to the present day, fear has been harnessed to rally support, justify policies, and maintain power. In the early days of human civilization, leaders often leveraged fear of external threats to unite communities and establish authority. In modern times, fear is strategically employed in media and political campaigns to manipulate emotions and steer public opinion towards desired outcomes. This manipulation of fear can lead to polarization, division, and the erosion of trust in institutions. While fear can be a powerful motivator, its unchecked use in political discourse can have detrimental effects on social cohesion and democratic principles. Therefore, it is imperative for leaders to wield fear responsibly and ethically, considering the long-term consequences of stoking fear for short-term gains. The use of fear in political discourse must be approached with caution and integrity to ensure a healthy and informed society.

Fear-mongering as a political strategy

In the world of politics, fear-mongering has been utilized as a strategic tool to sway public opinion and manipulate voters for centuries. By exploiting people's fears and insecurities, politicians can create a sense of urgency and crisis that allows them to push their agenda forward. This tactic is often seen as a way to control the narrative and divert attention from real issues, ultimately leading to a more polarized and divided society. Fear-mongering as a political strategy can be particularly damaging as it preys on people's emotions rather than rational thinking, leading to impulsive decision-making and the erosion of trust in government institutions. While fear can be a powerful motivator, it is crucial for voters to remain vigilant and discerning, questioning the validity and intentions behind the messages they are receiving. By promoting fear-based narratives, politicians risk undermining democracy and perpetuating a culture of division and mistrust.

Political policies and public fear

The intertwining of political policies and public fear creates a landscape of complex dynamics that often shape societal attitudes and behaviors. Political leaders have historically used fear as a tool to mobilize support for their agendas, whether through invoking threats from external enemies or emphasizing internal dangers. This manipulation of fear can lead to a heightened sense of insecurity among the public, which in turn can influence the decisions they make at the polls. The challenge lies in striking a balance between acknowledging legitimate concerns and preventing the exploitation of fear for political gain. When policies are driven by fear rather than reason, there is a risk of eroding civil liberties, stoking division, and impeding progress. Therefore, it is crucial for political leaders to approach policymaking with a commitment to addressing genuine threats while fostering a climate of transparency, trust, and rational deliberation. By recognizing the impact of fear on public perception and engagement, policymakers can work towards promoting a more informed and resilient society.

XVI. Fear and Economics

Throughout history, fear has played a crucial role in shaping economic behavior and decision-making. The XVI century, in particular, was marked by widespread fear of economic collapse, leading to various measures being implemented to stabilize markets. This fear of financial instability not only affected individual investors but also influenced governmental policies and international trade agreements. The fear of economic downturns can create a self-fulfilling prophecy, as people's anxiety can lead to hoarding resources, causing scarcity and further economic decline. However, fear can also serve as a driving force for innovation and adaptation, prompting individuals and societies to seek out new opportunities and mitigate risks. By understanding the psychology behind fear and economics, policymakers can better navigate economic challenges and promote sustainable growth. In this way, fear can be harnessed as a tool for progress rather than a hindrance to development.

Economic consequences of fear

Throughout history, fear has played a crucial role in shaping human behavior and decision-making processes, especially in economic contexts. The economic consequences of fear are manifold, impacting consumer behavior, investment decisions, and overall market volatility. When faced with uncertainty or perceived threats, individuals tend to adopt more conservative spending habits, leading to a decrease in consumer confidence and a slowdown in economic growth. Furthermore, fear can trigger panic selling in financial markets, resulting in sharp declines in asset prices and increased market instability. In extreme cases, widespread fear can even lead to banking crises and recessionary spirals. However, fear can also have positive economic effects, such as driving innovation and prompting governments to implement necessary reforms to mitigate risks. Thus, while fear can hinder economic progress, it can also serve as a catalyst for positive change and long-term growth if properly managed and leveraged.

Fear-driven market behaviors

In examining the fear-driven market behaviors, it becomes evident that the primal instinct of fear can lead to irrational decision-making in economic contexts. When individuals are driven by fear, whether it be fear of loss or fear of missing out, they tend to make impulsive and emotionally charged choices that may not align with their long-term financial goals. This can result in market volatility, bubbles, and crashes that have far-reaching consequences for the economy as a whole. While fear can motivate individuals to take action and protect their interests, it can also cloud judgment and lead to poor investments or panic selling. By understanding the psychological underpinnings of fear and learning to manage it through rational analysis and strategic decision-making, investors can navigate turbulent market conditions with more confidence and resilience. Ultimately, mastering fear in the realm of finance requires a balance between acknowledging its influence and maintaining a disciplined approach to managing risk.

Fear and consumer behavior

Through a combination of evolutionary biology and modern psychology, it is evident that fear plays a significant role in shaping consumer behavior. From an evolutionary standpoint, fear was developed as a survival mechanism to protect us from immediate threats. This primal instinct still influences how we perceive and respond to potential dangers in our environment, including in the realm of consumer choices. When faced with uncertain or risky decisions, fear can trigger a fight-or-flight response, leading individuals to make more conservative or risk-averse choices. However, with the rise of consumer culture and marketing tactics, fear can also be manipulated to evoke specific emotions and drive purchasing behavior. Marketers often use fear appeals to create a sense of urgency or scarcity, urging consumers to act quickly out of fear of missing out. Understanding the interplay between fear and consumer behavior is essential in navigating the complex landscape of modern marketing strategies and making informed choices as consumers. By recognizing the influence of fear on our decision-making processes, individuals can empower themselves to resist impulsive urges and make more rational and deliberate choices.

XVII. Fear and Healthcare

Ultimately, when considering the intersection of fear and healthcare, it is clear that fear can play a significant role in how individuals approach their own well-being. Fear, when understood and managed effectively, can serve as a motivator for seeking preventative care, adhering to treatment plans, and making healthier lifestyle choices. However, fear can also act as a barrier to accessing healthcare services, leading individuals to delay seeking medical attention out of anxiety or apprehension. It is imperative for healthcare providers to recognize the impact of fear on their patients' behavior and work towards creating a supportive and understanding environment that encourages open communication and trust. By addressing and alleviating patients' fears, healthcare professionals can enhance patient outcomes and promote overall well-being. In this way, fear in the context of healthcare must be acknowledged, understood, and effectively managed to ensure optimal health outcomes for all individuals.

Fear in medical settings

In medical settings, fear can manifest in various ways, impacting both patients and healthcare providers. Patients often experience fear due to the uncertainty of their condition, the potential for pain or discomfort, and the fear of the unknown outcomes of medical procedures. This fear can lead to increased stress levels, compromised decision-making abilities, and even avoidance of medical care altogether. Healthcare providers, on the other hand, may experience fear related to making mistakes, facing medical emergencies, or dealing with difficult patients. This fear can result in burnout, decreased job satisfaction, and ultimately, compromised patient care. Recognizing and addressing fear in medical settings is crucial for optimizing patient outcomes and improving the overall quality of healthcare delivery. By implementing strategies such as clear communication, empathy, and mindfulness techniques, both patients and healthcare providers can better manage their fears and work towards a more positive and effective medical experience.

Fear-related health disorders

In examining fear-related health disorders, it becomes evident that the implications extend beyond mere psychological distress to encompass a range of physical ailments as well. The physiological response to fear, known as the 'fight or flight' response, triggers a cascade of hormonal reactions that can have detrimental effects on the body if sustained over prolonged periods. Chronic fear and anxiety have been linked to increased risks of cardiovascular disease, weakened immune function, and even premature aging. Therefore, it is imperative to address not only the emotional aspects of fear but also its impact on overall health and well-being. By understanding the interconnectedness of mind and body, individuals can approach fear-related health disorders holistically, incorporating both psychological interventions and lifestyle changes to mitigate the negative consequences of chronic fear. In doing so, we can strive towards a more integrated approach to managing fear and promoting overall health and resilience.

Managing fear in healthcare environments

Therefore, in healthcare environments, managing fear is crucial for both medical professionals and patients. For healthcare providers, the high-stress nature of the job can lead to increased anxiety and fear, potentially impacting their ability to make sound decisions and provide optimal care. By implementing techniques such as mindfulness, deep breathing exercises, and mental visualization, healthcare workers can learn to regulate their fear response in stressful situations. Additionally, creating a supportive work environment where professionals feel safe to express their fears and seek help can also play a significant role in managing fear in healthcare settings. For patients, fear and anxiety are often associated with medical procedures, diagnosis, and hospital stays. Healthcare providers should take into consideration the psychological impact of fear on patients' well-being and implement strategies to help alleviate their anxiety, such as providing adequate information, emotional support, and a compassionate bedside manner. Overall, by recognizing the importance of managing fear in healthcare environments and implementing effective strategies to address it, both medical professionals and patients can experience improved outcomes and quality of care.

XVIII. Fear and Education

Furthermore, education plays a crucial role in helping individuals overcome their fears and anxieties. By arming ourselves with knowledge and understanding, we can combat the irrationality often associated with fear. Education provides us with tools to assess situations objectively, identify potential threats, and develop strategies to address them effectively. It empowers us to confront our fears head-on, rather than succumbing to them. Through education, we can learn coping mechanisms, stress management techniques, and mindfulness practices that can aid in managing fear and anxiety. Additionally, education fosters resilience by instilling confidence and self-efficacy in individuals, enabling them to face challenges with a greater sense of control and determination. By integrating fear education into curricula and promoting emotional intelligence development, we can cultivate a society that is better equipped to navigate the complexities of fear and emerge stronger and more resilient in the face of adversity.

The role of fear in educational settings

Fear in educational settings plays a multifaceted role that can both hinder and enhance learning. While some level of fear can serve as a motivator, pushing individuals to strive for success and excel in their academic pursuits, excessive fear can have detrimental effects. When students are overwhelmed by fear, whether it be fear of failure, fear of judgment from peers, or fear of not meeting expectations, their cognitive abilities are impaired, hindering their ability to absorb and retain information. Additionally, fear can lead to heightened stress levels, negatively impacting mental and physical health. Therefore, it is essential for educators to create a safe and supportive learning environment that encourages risk-taking and experimentation, helping students to overcome their fears and reach their full potential. By addressing and alleviating fear in educational settings, we can foster a positive and productive learning experience for all students.

Fear as a barrier to learning

In the intricate interplay between fear and learning, fear often acts as a formidable barrier that inhibits our ability to acquire new knowledge and skills. When faced with a daunting challenge or unfamiliar task, the physiological response to fear can trigger the instinctual fight-or-flight response, diverting cognitive resources away from active learning processes. This disruption hampers our capacity for logical reasoning and creative problem-solving, hindering our overall educational progress. Furthermore, fear can evoke a sense of anxiety or self-doubt, leading to avoidance behaviors that prevent us from fully engaging with educational opportunities. The impact of fear on learning outcomes underscores the importance of cultivating a supportive and nurturing environment that fosters resilience and encourages risk-taking. By acknowledging and addressing the role of fear as a barrier to learning, educators can implement strategies to alleviate student anxieties and promote a more conducive atmosphere for intellectual growth and development.

Strategies to overcome fear in education

Fear in education can be a significant barrier to learning, hindering academic progress and personal growth. To overcome this obstacle, strategies must be employed to help students manage and confront their fears effectively. One approach is to create a supportive and safe learning environment where students feel comfortable expressing their concerns and seeking help when needed. By fostering open communication and providing resources for mental health support, educators can help students address their fears head-on. Additionally, incorporating mindfulness and relaxation techniques into the curriculum can equip students with tools to reduce anxiety and increase focus during challenging tasks. Encouraging a growth mindset and resilience in the face of failure can also help students see fear as an opportunity for growth rather than a roadblock. By implementing these strategies, educators can empower students to overcome their fears and thrive in their educational journey.

XIX. Fear and Social Interactions

It is undeniable that fear plays a foundational role in shaping human social interactions. When confronted with unfamiliar situations or potential threats, individuals often experience a heightened sense of fear that can impact their behavior and interactions with others. This primal instinct, stemming from our evolutionary past, serves as a natural response to perceived danger, triggering a cascade of physiological and psychological responses aimed at self-preservation. However, the way in which fear manifests in social settings can be complex and multifaceted. Fear can create barriers to communication and collaboration, leading to misunderstandings and conflicts. On the other hand, fear can also serve as a motivator for individuals to bond together, forming tight-knit communities based on shared experiences and mutual support in the face of adversity. Therefore, understanding the nuances of fear in social interactions is crucial for navigating the complexities of human relationships and fostering a sense of unity and resilience in society.

Fear in social relationships

Throughout human history, fear has played a pivotal role in shaping social relationships. From tribal warfare to modern politics, fear has been utilized as a tool to control and manipulate others. The beginning of this manipulation can be seen in the early stages of civilization, where leaders would instill fear in their subjects to maintain power and authority. This manipulation of fear can be seen in contemporary society as well, with media, politicians, and even individuals using fear to sway public opinion and behavior. The power of fear in social relationships lies in its ability to tap into our primal instincts, and when left unchecked, it can lead to division, prejudice, and violence. In order to move beyond fear in social relationships, individuals must cultivate empathy, understanding, and critical thinking to counteract the negative impact of fear on human interactions. By recognizing and addressing the role of fear in social dynamics, we can strive towards more inclusive and cooperative communities built on trust and respect.

Fear of rejection and its social implications

It is evident that the fear of rejection holds significant social implications, shaping the way individuals interact and form relationships in society. This fear can lead to a reluctance to put oneself out there, diminishing opportunities for personal growth and connection with others. Furthermore, the fear of rejection can foster a sense of isolation and loneliness, hindering one's ability to engage authentically with the world around them. Consequently, individuals may develop defense mechanisms or coping strategies to avoid facing rejection, perpetuating a cycle of avoidance and potential missed opportunities for social connection. As such, it is crucial for individuals to recognize and address this fear, seeking support and guidance to overcome its grip. By confronting the fear of rejection head-on, individuals can cultivate resilience, self-acceptance, and healthier social interactions, ultimately enriching their lives and contributing positively to their communities.

Overcoming social fears

Fear, a primal instinct deeply ingrained in the human psyche, serves as a protective mechanism vital for survival. However, in modern society, social fears can often hinder individual growth and limit opportunities for personal development. Overcoming these fears requires a conscious effort to challenge oneself and gradually expose oneself to uncomfortable situations. By utilizing techniques such as systematic desensitization and cognitive-behavioral therapy, individuals can learn to confront and ultimately conquer their social anxieties. Through repeated exposure and practice, individuals can rewire their brains to respond differently to fear-inducing stimuli, paving the way for personal growth and increased self-confidence. By mastering social fears, individuals can unlock their full potential, fostering stronger relationships, advancing in their careers, and living more fulfilling lives. It is through facing our social fears head-on that we can truly break free from the constraints that hold us back and embrace the limitless possibilities that await us.

XX. Fear and Personal Development

Exploring the intersection of fear and personal development unveils a crucial aspect of human evolution and survival. Fear, as a deeply ingrained instinct, serves as a protective mechanism to shield us from harm and danger. This primal response has been honed over millennia to ensure the survival of our species, demonstrating its undeniable importance in our existence. However, the key lies in understanding how to harness and control this fear, especially in high-stress situations where clear thinking and calm demeanor are essential. By delving into psychological and physical techniques, individuals can equip themselves with the tools to confront and conquer their fears. Through gradual exposure and systematic desensitization, one can learn to navigate the murky waters of anxiety and emerge stronger on the other side. Ultimately, mastering fear not only enhances physical survivability but also enriches one's quality of life, leading to greater resilience and self-awareness. Embracing fear as a companion rather than a foe paves the way for personal growth and development, showcasing its profound impact on human flourishing.

Fear as a motivator for personal growth

The interplay between fear and personal growth is a fascinating one, rooted in the innate instinct for survival that has guided human behavior for millennia. As humans, we are hardwired to respond to threats with fear, triggering a cascade of physiological and psychological responses that prepare us to fight or flee. This primal fear can act as a powerful motivator for personal growth when channeled effectively. By confronting our fears head-on, we push ourselves outside of our comfort zones and challenge our limitations, leading to personal development and growth. Whether it's overcoming a fear of public speaking or facing a phobia, each step taken towards conquering fear builds resilience and self-confidence. This process of confronting and overcoming fear not only leads to personal growth but also enhances our ability to navigate life's challenges with courage and grace. In essence, fear, when harnessed and managed effectively, can be a catalyst for profound personal transformation and growth.

Fear and self-awareness

It is through the lens of fear that true self-awareness can be achieved. When faced with a threat or danger, our instinctual fear response is triggered in order to protect us. This innate re-action forces us to confront our vulnerabilities and weaknesses, leading to a deeper understanding of ourselves. Through intro-spection and reflection on our fear responses, we can uncover our deepest fears and insecurities, gaining insights into our own psyche. By acknowledging and accepting our fears, we can begin to develop strategies to overcome them, leading to per-sonal growth and self-improvement. This self-awareness allows us to recognize our limitations and strengths, enabling us to navigate challenging situations with a sense of calm and clarity. In essence, fear serves as a catalyst for self-discovery and in-trospection, pushing us to confront our innermost thoughts and emotions in order to become more resilient and self-aware in-dividuals.

Techniques for using fear to enhance personal development

Mastering fear can be a powerful tool for personal development when approached strategically and intentionally. By utilizing techniques such as visualization, mindfulness, and controlled exposure, individuals can gradually desensitize themselves to fear-inducing stimuli, thus enhancing their ability to confront and overcome challenges. For example, athletes often use visualization to mentally rehearse high-pressure situations, reducing anxiety and improving performance. Similarly, mindfulness practices can help individuals stay present and focused in the face of fear, allowing them to make rational decisions rather than succumbing to panic. Additionally, gradual exposure to feared situations or stimuli can help retrain the brain's response, ultimately leading to decreased fear and increased confidence. By incorporating these techniques into their personal development journey, individuals can harness fear as a motivator for growth, resilience, and self-improvement. Through intentional practice and perseverance, fear can be transformed from a hindrance into a catalyst for personal transformation.

XXI. Fear and Leadership

Throughout history, fear has played a significant role in shaping leadership dynamics. Leaders who could effectively manage their fears were often perceived as strong and capable, inspiring loyalty and confidence among their followers. From warriors facing battle to modern-day CEOs making tough business decisions, fear has been a driving force behind leadership actions. However, the line between courage and recklessness can be blurred when fear is not properly understood and controlled. Effective leaders must confront their fears head-on, acknowledging their presence without allowing them to dictate their decisions. Those who can navigate the delicate balance between acknowledging fear as a natural response and not succumbing to its paralyzing effects are more likely to inspire trust and lead their teams through uncertainty. Therefore, in the realm of leadership, fear can be both a hindrance and a powerful tool when managed wisely.

The impact of fear on leadership styles

Fear, while primarily an instinctual response, can deeply influence the style of leadership a person adopts. When leaders are driven by fear, their decisions tend to be reactive, short-sighted, and often focused on self-preservation rather than the greater good. This can result in a leadership style that is authoritarian, controlling, and lacking in empathy. Fear-based leaders may resort to intimidation, manipulation, and coercion to maintain power and control, breeding a toxic work environment characterized by distrust and insecurity. On the other hand, when leaders approach their roles with courage, confidence, and a willingness to confront their fears, they can inspire trust, empower their team members, and foster a culture of collaboration and innovation. By acknowledging and managing their fears, leaders can cultivate a leadership style that is grounded in authenticity, integrity, and a genuine commitment to the well-being of their followers. Ultimately, the impact of fear on leadership styles underscores the importance of self-awareness, emotional intelligence, and the ability to transcend one's personal fears in order to lead effectively and ethically.

Overcoming fear to become an effective leader

In the realm of leadership, the ability to overcome fear is not just a desirable trait but a crucial one. Effective leaders are those who can manage their fears and anxieties, remaining clear-headed and composed in the face of adversity. By mastering their fears, leaders can make rational decisions, inspire confidence in their team, and navigate challenges with grace and resilience. This requires a deep understanding of one's own fears and triggers, as well as the willingness to confront them head-on. Through practice, training, and self-reflection, leaders can learn to harness their fears as a source of strength rather than weakness. They can use fear as a motivator to push boundaries, take calculated risks, and achieve greatness. Ultimately, by overcoming fear, leaders can unlock their full potential and become a beacon of inspiration and guidance for others. Fear, when understood and controlled, can be a powerful tool for personal and professional growth.

Case studies of leadership under fear

It is intriguing to examine the various case studies of leadership under fear, as they offer valuable insights into how individuals can navigate and overcome challenges when faced with danger or uncertainty. One such case study that stands out is that of Nelson Mandela, who demonstrated remarkable leadership during his imprisonment by the apartheid regime in South Africa. Despite enduring years of fear, isolation, and oppression, Mandela maintained his composure, resilience, and strategic thinking, ultimately leading to his eventual release and the dismantling of apartheid. His ability to channel fear into motivation and action serves as a powerful example of effective leadership under extreme circumstances. By studying such examples of leadership under fear, we can glean valuable lessons on how to harness our own fear responses in order to make informed decisions, inspire others, and achieve positive outcomes in challenging situations.

XXII. Fear and Decision Making

In the realm of decision-making, fear plays a significant role that cannot be overlooked. When faced with a situation that triggers fear, our natural instinct is to either fight, flight, or freeze. This primal response is deeply ingrained in our biology as a means of survival, helping us react quickly to potential threats. However, the evolution of human cognition has allowed us to transcend mere instinct and incorporate reasoning into our decision-making process. By analyzing and understanding the source of our fears, we can empower ourselves to make more informed, rational choices. Furthermore, through exposure therapy and other psychological techniques, individuals can learn to confront and overcome their fears, ultimately leading to a greater sense of self-mastery and control. It is through this balance of fear and reason that we can navigate the complexities of decision-making, utilizing our primal instincts as a catalyst for growth and self-improvement.

Fear's impact on rational decision-making

Fear, often considered an obstructive force in rational decision-making, actually plays a crucial role in human survival. In the face of danger, fear triggers the fight-or-flight response, mobilizing the body to respond to threats efficiently. While fear can lead to impulsive reactions, it can also serve as a powerful motivator for strategic planning and careful consideration of potential risks. By acknowledging and understanding our fears, we can harness their energy to make informed decisions that prioritize safety and well-being. Through a combination of biological instincts and cognitive reasoning, individuals can navigate challenging circumstances with resilience and composure. By recognizing fear as a natural aspect of human experience, we can cultivate a balanced approach that incorporates both instinct and reason in our decision-making processes, ultimately leading to enhanced survival outcomes and personal growth. Fear, when managed effectively, can be transformed from a hindrance to a valuable asset in the pursuit of optimal decision-making.

Strategies to mitigate fear's influence on decisions

Within the realm of decision-making, fear can play a significant role in influencing the outcomes of choices. In order to mitigate fear's impact on decisions, individuals can employ various strategies to maintain a rational and clear perspective. One effective approach is to engage in mindfulness practices, such as meditation or deep breathing exercises, to cultivate a sense of calm and focus amidst fear-inducing scenarios. Additionally, seeking support from trusted confidants or mental health professionals can provide valuable insights and guidance in processing and addressing underlying fears that may be clouding judgment. Another strategy is to practice visualization techniques, envisioning successful outcomes and mentally preparing for potential obstacles, which can help reduce anxiety and boost confidence in decision-making. By implementing these strategies to manage fear, individuals can enhance their ability to make sound and reasoned choices, even in the face of uncertainty and adversity.

Decision-making models that account for fear

Throughout history, decision-making models that account for fear have played a crucial role in human survival. The primal instinct of fear has been a driving force behind the development of strategies to assess risks and make educated choices. Understanding fear as a natural response to danger allows individuals to acknowledge its presence without succumbing to its paralyzing effects. By incorporating fear into decision-making models, individuals can better assess threats, weigh risks, and choose the most appropriate course of action. However, it is essential to strike a balance between instinctual fear and rational reasoning. Recognizing the role fear plays in decision-making can empower individuals to confront their fears, learn to manage them effectively, and ultimately lead to better outcomes in challenging situations. By integrating fear into decision-making processes, individuals can harness its power to enhance their survival instincts and navigate complex scenarios with resilience and clarity.

XXIII. Fear and Risk Management

Ultimately, fear and risk management go hand in hand in the realm of human survival. While fear is a natural response designed to protect us from danger, it is crucial to understand how to control and mitigate it in various situations. Trained individuals, such as firefighters and soldiers, exemplify how mastering fear can lead to effective performance under pressure. Techniques like gradual exposure and systematic desensitization are invaluable tools in confronting and overcoming fears. By repeatedly facing fears, individuals can build resilience and improve their ability to stay calm and clear-headed in high-stress scenarios. This not only enhances physical survival but also contributes to a higher quality of life. Viewing fear as a valuable ally rather than an enemy is key to developing self-awareness and inner strength. Through a combination of biological responses and psychological strategies, fear and risk management play a vital role in navigating the challenges of human existence.

Fear in risk assessment

Through an understanding of the evolutionary purpose of fear, we come to recognize its intrinsic role in the human experience. Our instincts to fear dangerous situations and react swiftly have been pivotal in our survival as a species. However, in the modern world, where the threats have transformed and diversified, the ability to assess risks accurately becomes paramount. Fear, although necessary, can sometimes cloud our judgment and lead to irrational decisions that may not be in our best interest. It is essential, therefore, to strike a balance between acknowledging fear as a valuable indicator of potential danger while also maintaining a rational and logical approach to risk assessment. By combining our innate instincts with informed reasoning and utilizing available resources, we can navigate through life's challenges with a greater sense of control and resilience. Ultimately, mastering fear in risk assessment is not about eliminating the emotion entirely, but rather harnessing it as a tool for informed decision-making and enhanced survival.

Balancing fear and risk in decision-making

As individuals navigate through the complexities of decision-making, striking a balance between fear and risk becomes paramount. The natural instinct of fear, honed by evolution to ensure survival, often leads individuals to perceive risks as greater than they may actually be. However, by applying reason and critical thinking, individuals can recalibrate their responses to fear, enabling them to make more informed decisions. Trained professionals, such as firefighters and soldiers, exemplify how mastering fear can enhance performance in high-stress situations. Through psychological and physical techniques, anyone can cultivate the ability to remain calm and focused under pressure. Confronting fears gradually, through methods like exposure therapy, allows individuals to build resilience and overcome debilitating anxieties. In essence, balancing fear and risk in decision-making requires a blend of instinctual responses and rational analysis to navigate life's challenges effectively.

Risk management techniques to alleviate fear

The utilization of risk management techniques is crucial in alleviating fear and promoting effective decision-making in high-stress situations. By implementing strategies such as risk assessment, contingency planning, and crisis communication, individuals can proactively identify potential threats and develop appropriate responses to mitigate their impact. Additionally, the establishment of clear protocols and guidelines for responding to emergencies can help to instill a sense of control and confidence, reducing feelings of helplessness and anxiety. Through the application of risk management principles, individuals can enhance their ability to remain calm and composed when faced with fear-inducing scenarios, enabling them to make rational choices based on facts and evidence rather than emotions. Ultimately, by mastering these techniques, individuals can navigate challenging circumstances with resilience and effectiveness, transcending the limitations imposed by fear and increasing their capacity for survival and success.

XXIV. Fear and Crisis Management

Throughout history, fear has played a vital role in human survival, signaling danger and mobilizing our bodies to respond accordingly. As we have evolved, so too has our ability to manage and control fear in times of crisis. Trained professionals, such as first responders and military personnel, undergo extensive training to learn how to navigate high-stress situations with composure and clarity. By utilizing techniques like controlled breathing, visualization, and cognitive restructuring, individuals can override their instinctual fear responses and make rational decisions in the face of danger. Moreover, the process of facing fears head-on through exposure therapy allows individuals to gradually desensitize themselves to their triggers, ultimately reducing their fear responses over time. By mastering fear, not only can individuals enhance their physical survival in times of crisis, but they can also achieve a higher quality of life by cultivating resilience and self-awareness. Fear, when understood and managed effectively, can be transformed from a hindrance into a powerful ally in the journey of human survival and growth.

Role of fear in emergency responses

Mastering fear is crucial in emergency responses as it can determine the outcome of a high-stress situation. Through training and experience, individuals can learn to control their instinctual reactions to fear, allowing them to think rationally and act decisively when faced with danger. By utilizing psychological and physical techniques, such as deep breathing exercises and mental visualization, individuals can maintain a sense of calm and focus amidst chaos. Moreover, confronting fears in a systematic and controlled manner can help individuals overcome phobias and anxieties, ultimately increasing their resilience in the face of adversity. It is essential to view fear not as a hindrance, but as a tool that can be harnessed for self-improvement and growth. By understanding the role of fear in emergency responses and learning to manage it effectively, individuals can enhance their ability to navigate challenging situations with courage and composure.

Training for fear management in crises

In the context of managing fear in crises, training plays a crucial role in equipping individuals with the necessary skills to respond effectively under pressure. By exposing individuals to simulated fear-inducing scenarios, training programs aim to desensitize them to the physiological and psychological effects of fear. This exposure enables individuals to develop coping mechanisms and strategies to remain calm and focused in high-stress situations. Moreover, training instills a sense of confidence and competence, empowering individuals to confront fears head-on rather than succumb to panic or paralysis. Through structured training modules that combine physical and mental exercises, individuals can gradually learn to override their instinctual fear responses with rational and deliberate actions. Ultimately, training for fear management in crises is about promoting resilience, adaptability, and sound decision-making in the face of adversity, ensuring that individuals can navigate through challenging circumstances with confidence and composure.

Case studies of crisis management involving fear

In examining case studies of crisis management involving fear, it becomes evident that the ability to control this powerful emotion can be a determining factor in survival. Individuals facing life-threatening situations often experience a surge of fear that can cloud judgment and hinder decision-making. However, through training and experience, individuals can learn to harness their fear, using it as a source of energy and focus rather than a paralyzing force. For example, firefighters undergo rigorous training to confront their fears head-on, enabling them to perform effectively in high-stress situations. Similarly, soldiers are trained to manage their fear in combat, allowing them to carry out their mission with precision and clarity. By studying these case studies and the strategies employed by those who successfully manage fear, individuals can learn valuable skills to navigate crises with composure and resilience. Ultimately, mastering fear is not about eliminating it entirely, but rather about understanding its role and learning to work alongside it in moments of crisis.

XXV. Fear and Military Training

In the realm of military training, fear plays a pivotal role in shaping the behavior and performance of soldiers in high-stress environments. Acknowledging fear as a natural response crucial for survival, military institutions have developed rigorous training programs to help recruits confront and control their fears effectively. Through simulated combat scenarios, intense physical challenges, and mental conditioning, soldiers are trained to navigate fear-induced instincts and maintain composure under pressure. This training not only bolsters their ability to make sound decisions in the face of danger but also cultivates resilience and adaptability in the field. By exposing recruits to controlled doses of fear and equipping them with the tools to manage their emotional responses, military training harnesses fear as a catalyst for developing disciplined and effective warriors capable of operating in the most demanding circumstances.

Fear management techniques in military training

Fear management techniques in military training involve a combination of psychological and physical strategies to help soldiers cope with intense and potentially life-threatening situations. These techniques are crucial for ensuring that soldiers can perform effectively under pressure, remain calm, and make rational decisions amidst chaos. One such approach is exposure therapy, where soldiers are gradually exposed to fear-inducing stimuli in a controlled environment to desensitize them to their triggers. This method helps them build resilience and develop the mental fortitude needed to face their fears head-on. Additionally, mindfulness practices and breathing exercises are taught to help soldiers regulate their emotions and stay focused in high-stress situations. By mastering fear, soldiers can enhance their performance, maintain situational awareness, and ultimately increase their chances of survival in combat scenarios. Through rigorous training and the implementation of fear management techniques, military personnel can harness fear as a source of strength rather than allowing it to paralyze them.

The role of fear in combat situations

In the complex and high-stakes environment of combat situations, fear plays a crucial role in influencing human behavior. Fear, as a primal instinct, triggers the body's fight-or-flight response, preparing individuals to either confront the threat or flee from danger. This automatic reaction can be both beneficial and detrimental in combat scenarios, as it heightens awareness and boosts physical capabilities, but can also lead to panic and impaired decision-making. However, through training and experience, individuals can learn to harness fear as a source of strength rather than weakness. By understanding how fear operates on a biological and psychological level, combatants can develop strategies to manage their emotions, stay focused, and act rationally under pressure. Thus, fear in combat situations can be seen not as a hindrance, but as a powerful tool that, when mastered, can enhance performance and increase the chances of survival.

Psychological support for soldiers dealing with fear

The psychological support for soldiers dealing with fear is a critical component of their overall well-being and effectiveness in the field. Soldiers facing extreme situations are often exposed to high levels of stress and fear, which can impact their decision-making abilities and performance. By providing soldiers with access to trained therapists and counselors who can help them navigate their fears, the military can ensure that these individuals are better equipped to cope with the challenges they face. Additionally, implementing strategies such as cognitive-behavioral therapy and mindfulness techniques can aid soldiers in managing their fear responses and maintaining a sense of calm under pressure. Ultimately, investing in psychological support for soldiers not only enhances their individual resilience and mental health but also contributes to the overall success of military operations. By recognizing the importance of addressing the psychological needs of soldiers, we can support their well-being and optimize their performance in the field.

XXVI. Fear and Law Enforcement

Fear not only plays a crucial role in individual survival but also in shaping societal structures, particularly in the context of law enforcement. The enforcement of laws and maintenance of social order rely heavily on fear as a deterrent against criminal behavior. The fear of consequences such as imprisonment or fines acts as a powerful motivator for individuals to abide by societal norms and regulations. However, there is a fine line between utilizing fear as a tool for maintaining order and allowing fear to drive authoritarian or oppressive practices within law enforcement agencies. The misuse of fear can lead to abuses of power, violations of civil rights, and erode public trust in the justice system. Therefore, it is essential for law enforcement officials to understand the psychology of fear, both in themselves and the communities they serve, in order to strike a balance between ensuring safety and upholding justice. By acknowledging and addressing the role of fear in law enforcement, society can work towards creating a more equitable and just system that effectively protects and serves its citizens.

Fear in policing and law enforcement tactics

In the context of law enforcement and policing tactics, fear can play a crucial role in how officers approach their duties. The fear of danger or harm can lead to a heightened sense of alertness and readiness to respond to potential threats, which can be essential when dealing with unpredictable or violent situations. However, this fear, if not properly managed or understood, can also lead to negative outcomes such as overreactions or unnecessary use of force. Therefore, it is imperative for law enforcement agencies to provide adequate training and resources to help officers effectively navigate their fears in the line of duty. By combining instinctual responses with rational decision-making processes, officers can strike a balance that allows them to protect themselves and others while upholding the principles of justice and fairness. Ultimately, acknowledging and addressing fear in policing can lead to safer communities and more effective law enforcement practices overall.

Training law enforcement to handle fear

Through proper training and preparation, law enforcement officers can learn to handle fear in high-stress situations more effectively. By providing officers with psychological techniques, physical training, and real-life scenarios to practice in controlled environments, they can develop the skills needed to remain calm and focused when faced with danger. This type of training not only enhances officer safety but also improves the outcomes of critical incidents by enabling them to make better decisions under pressure. Additionally, by understanding the physiological responses to fear and learning how to manage them, law enforcement officers can avoid unnecessary escalation and uphold the principles of de-escalation in their interactions with the public. Ultimately, training law enforcement to handle fear is essential for promoting a safer and more effective approach to policing that prioritizes both officer and community well-being.

Impact of fear on law enforcement decision-making

When considering the impact of fear on law enforcement decision-making, it becomes evident that this primal instinct plays a crucial role in shaping the actions of those in positions of authority. Fear can lead to a heightened state of alertness, increased vigilance, and quick decision-making in dangerous situations. However, fear can also cloud judgment and lead to impulsive or aggressive actions that may not align with the principles of justice and fairness. Law enforcement officers must undergo thorough training to learn how to manage their fear responses effectively, ensuring that they can act in a manner that upholds the law while prioritizing the safety of themselves and others. By understanding the psychological effects of fear on decision-making processes, law enforcement agencies can develop strategies and protocols to mitigate its negative impact and ensure that officers are equipped to handle high-stress situations with professionalism and integrity.

XXVII. Fear and Extreme Sports

In the realm of extreme sports, fear plays a crucial role in the heightened experiences that participants seek. It is not fear itself that is the enemy, but its mismanagement that can lead to disastrous consequences. Extreme athletes harness fear as a tool, utilizing the adrenaline rush to enhance their performance and push their limits. By confronting their fears head-on, they develop a deep understanding of their own capabilities and limitations. However, the fine line between exhilaration and danger must be carefully treaded, as unchecked fear can lead to reckless decisions and potentially life-threatening situations. Through rigorous training and mental fortitude, extreme sports enthusiasts learn to channel their fear into a source of motivation and focus, allowing them to navigate extreme environments with precision and skill. Ultimately, fear in extreme sports serves as a paradoxical force – both thrilling and potentially lethal – highlighting the delicate balance between instinct and reason in the pursuit of adrenaline-fueled challenges.

Fear as a component of extreme sports

Fear plays a significant role in extreme sports, serving as a vital component that heightens the thrill and excitement of these activities. As individuals engage in high-risk adventures such as skydiving or rock climbing, fear acts as a motivator, pushing them to overcome their limitations and conquer their anxieties. The adrenaline rush that accompanies fear can increase focus and agility, allowing athletes to perform at their peak. However, it is essential to strike a balance between fear and control in extreme sports to prevent reckless behavior that can lead to accidents. Athletes must learn to harness their fear, using it to enhance their performance rather than allowing it to impair their judgment. By understanding the role of fear in extreme sports and learning to manage it effectively, athletes can push their boundaries while still prioritizing safety and well-being. In this way, fear becomes a valuable tool that contributes to the exhilaration and challenge of extreme sports without compromising the overall experience.

Managing fear for performance in extreme conditions

In the realm of managing fear for performance in extreme conditions, the ability to maintain composure and clarity becomes paramount. While fear is a natural response designed to protect us from danger, it can also hinder our ability to perform effectively in high-stress situations. Trained individuals such as firefighters and soldiers exemplify how fear can be managed through a combination of psychological techniques and physical training. By confronting fears gradually and utilizing strategies like systematic desensitization, individuals can learn to overcome their natural instinctive responses and remain calm under pressure. This process not only enhances one's performance in extreme conditions but also fosters self-awareness and resilience. Ultimately, mastering fear is not about eradicating it, but understanding its role as an ally in navigating challenges and pushing the boundaries of human potential. Through a combination of training, practice, and self-reflection, individuals can learn to harness fear as a source of strength rather than a limitation.

Psychological traits of extreme sports athletes

In understanding the psychological traits of extreme sports athletes, it becomes evident that these individuals possess a unique combination of characteristics that set them apart from the average person. Research suggests that many extreme sports athletes exhibit high levels of sensation-seeking behavior, a trait characterized by a need for novel and intense experiences. This propensity for seeking out adrenaline-pumping activities may indicate a higher tolerance for risk and a greater ability to manage fear and anxiety in high-pressure situations. Additionally, studies have shown that extreme sports athletes tend to have a heightened sense of autonomy and a strong internal locus of control, which allows them to navigate challenging environments with confidence and self-assurance. Furthermore, the intense focus and mental clarity required to excel in extreme sports suggest a high level of emotional regulation and cognitive control among these individuals. Overall, the psychological profile of extreme sports athletes reflects a unique blend of fearlessness, self-reliance, and resilience that enables them to thrive in the face of extreme challenges.

XXVIII. Fear and Performance Arts

Throughout history, fear has played a significant role in shaping human behavior and survival strategies. As fear is deeply ingrained in our biology, it serves as a powerful motivator for self-preservation. However, the relationship between fear and performance arts, such as acting or public speaking, is complex. On one hand, fear can hinder performance by causing anxiety and nervousness, leading to a lack of focus and confidence. Yet, on the other hand, fear can also be a driving force behind powerful and emotive performances. Through harnessing fear, performers can tap into raw emotions and convey authenticity to their audiences. Moreover, the adrenaline rush induced by fear can enhance creativity and improvisation in the moment, leading to memorable and impactful performances. In this way, fear can be seen as a double-edged sword in the realm of performance arts, capable of both hindering and enhancing artistic expression.

Managing stage fright in performance arts

The mastery of fear in performance arts is a crucial skill for artists to develop in order to deliver their best work on stage. By understanding the physiological responses to fear, such as increased heart rate and shallow breathing, performers can employ techniques like mindfulness and visualization to calm their nerves before a performance. Additionally, practice and preparation play a key role in managing stage fright, as the more familiar a performer is with their material, the more confident they will feel on stage. Building a support network of peers and mentors can also provide emotional reassurance and guidance in navigating the pressures of performing. By blending the instinctual response to fear with reasoned strategies for managing it, artists can elevate their performances and connect more deeply with their audience, ultimately achieving a greater sense of artistic fulfillment.

Fear's role in creative expression

The complex interplay between fear and creative expression is a compelling facet of human psychology, shaping the way individuals approach artistic endeavors. Fear, often viewed as a hindrance to creativity, can actually serve as a catalyst for innovation and deeper self-exploration. When individuals are faced with fear, whether it be fear of failure, fear of judgment, or fear of the unknown, they are prompted to dig deeper within themselves for courage and resilience. This internal battle against fear can spark a surge of creativity, as individuals harness their emotions and vulnerabilities to create art that is raw, authentic, and impactful. In this way, fear not only challenges individuals to confront their innermost demons but also empowers them to channel these emotions into artistic expression that resonates with others on a profound level. Thus, fear's role in creative expression is a multifaceted one, shaping the very essence of human creativity and pushing individuals to transcend their limitations in pursuit of artistic excellence.

Techniques for performers to overcome fear

In the context of performing arts, fear can be a significant obstacle that hinders the ability of artists and performers to deliver their best work on stage. However, there are techniques that performers can employ to overcome this fear and deliver a powerful and captivating performance. One effective technique is mindfulness and visualization, where performers can mentally rehearse their performance and focus on positive outcomes to build confidence and reduce anxiety. Breathing exercises can also help calm the nervous system and center the mind before going on stage. Additionally, seeking feedback and support from peers and mentors can provide reassurance and encouragement, helping performers feel more prepared and confident. By incorporating these techniques into their practice routine, performers can effectively manage and conquer their fears, allowing their talent and creativity to shine through in their performances. By mastering these techniques, performers can leverage their fear as a driving force for excellence and artistic growth, enhancing their overall stage presence and impact on audiences.

XXIX. Fear and Public Speaking

Throughout human history, fear has served as a powerful evolutionary tool, helping our ancestors survive in hostile environments. However, in modern society, fear often manifests itself in unexpected ways – one of the most common being the fear of public speaking. Fear and Public Speaking elicits a strong physiological response rooted in ancient survival instincts, triggering the infamous fight-or-flight response. This fear can be debilitating, leading to anxiety, panic, and avoidance behaviors. Yet, as we delve deeper into the psychology of fear, we uncover techniques and strategies to combat this fear effectively. By utilizing rational thinking, systematic desensitization, and exposure therapy, individuals can gradually overcome their fear of public speaking and harness its energy to enhance their communication skills. Through understanding the evolutionary origins of fear and employing modern techniques, individuals can transform fear from a hindrance into a powerful tool for personal growth and development.

Common fears associated with public speaking

The innate fear of public speaking is a universal phenomenon that plagues many individuals, regardless of their background or experience. Beginning with the fear of judgment and rejection by an audience, this common phobia often stems from a deep-seated need for approval and validation. The fear of failure, whether in forgetting one's lines or stumbling over words, can lead to heightened anxiety and self-doubt. Additionally, the fear of being perceived as incompetent or unintelligent can exacerbate feelings of insecurity and inadequacy. These fears can be further compounded by the fear of losing credibility or authority in front of an audience, leading to a sense of vulnerability and exposure. In order to combat these fears associated with public speaking, individuals must cultivate self-confidence, practice effective communication techniques, and develop coping strategies to manage stage fright and anxiety. Through a combination of preparation, practice, and mindset shifts, individuals can overcome their fears and deliver compelling and impactful speeches with ease and poise.

Strategies to overcome fear of public speaking

In the quest to overcome the fear of public speaking, individuals can employ a variety of effective strategies. One approach involves thorough preparation, including practicing the speech multiple times and familiarizing oneself with the material to boost confidence and reduce anxiety. Furthermore, focusing on the message and the audience rather than personal fears can shift the focus away from self-doubt. Another strategy is to engage in relaxation techniques such as deep breathing or visualization exercises to calm the nerves before speaking. Additionally, seeking feedback from trusted individuals or joining public speaking groups can provide constructive criticism and support for improvement. Finally, gradual exposure to speaking in front of small groups can help desensitize individuals to the fear and build confidence over time. By implementing these strategies consistently, individuals can gradually overcome their fear of public speaking and become more effective and confident communicators.

Benefits of mastering public speaking fears

Throughout history, the ability to master one's fear of public speaking has been considered a valuable skill, especially in leadership roles and professions that require effective communication. One of the main benefits of conquering this fear is increased self-confidence. By overcoming the anxiety and nervousness associated with public speaking, individuals can build a stronger sense of self-assurance that permeates other aspects of their lives. Additionally, mastering public speaking fears can lead to improved professional opportunities. Those who can articulate ideas clearly and confidently are more likely to advance in their careers, as effective communication is highly valued in the workplace. Furthermore, conquering public speaking fears can enhance personal relationships by allowing individuals to express themselves more openly and authentically. By pushing past their fears and honing their communication skills, individuals can unlock new opportunities for growth and success in both their personal and professional lives.

XXX. Fear and Entrepreneurship

Throughout history, fear has played a crucial role in shaping human behavior, particularly when it comes to entrepreneurship. The fear of failure, financial loss, or being judged by others can be paralyzing for aspiring entrepreneurs. However, it is essential to recognize that fear is a natural response designed to protect us from potential threats. By acknowledging and understanding these fears, entrepreneurs can harness them as a source of motivation and drive. In fact, some of the most successful entrepreneurs credit their fear as a driving force behind their innovation and determination to succeed. By reframing fear as a challenge to be overcome rather than an insurmountable obstacle, entrepreneurs can cultivate resilience and persistence in the face of adversity. Embracing fear as a catalyst for growth can propel entrepreneurs towards achieving their goals and realizing their full potential in the competitive world of business.

Fear of failure in entrepreneurship

Throughout history, fear has been a primal instinct that has guided human survival, triggering the fight or flight response in the face of danger. This instinctual response is deeply ingrained in our biology, designed to protect us from threats that could potentially harm us. However, in the context of entrepreneurship, this fear of failure can be paralyzing, preventing individuals from taking risks and pursuing new ventures. The fear of failure in entrepreneurship is often rooted in the unknown outcomes and potential consequences of a business venture not succeeding. This fear can hinder innovation, creativity, and overall growth in the entrepreneurial landscape. While fear can be a powerful motivator in some situations, it must be managed effectively in order to navigate the uncertainties of the business world. By acknowledging and understanding this fear, entrepreneurs can develop strategies to overcome it, allowing them to take calculated risks and pursue their entrepreneurial dreams with confidence and resilience.

Overcoming entrepreneurial fears

When faced with the challenges of entrepreneurship, individuals often grapple with a multitude of fears that can hinder their success. These fears may range from the fear of failure and financial loss to the fear of rejection and criticism. However, overcoming these entrepreneurial fears is essential for personal growth and business development. One effective strategy for conquering these fears is through exposure therapy and cognitive behavioral techniques. By gradually facing and confronting their fears, entrepreneurs can desensitize themselves to the emotional responses that hold them back. Additionally, fostering a mindset of resilience and embracing failure as a learning opportunity can help individuals navigate the uncertainties of the entrepreneurial journey with courage and determination. Ultimately, by acknowledging and addressing their fears head-on, entrepreneurs can unlock their full potential and achieve their goals with confidence and clarity.

Case studies of successful entrepreneurs who managed fear

In exploring the complex relationship between fear and human survival, it is essential to examine case studies of successful entrepreneurs who have effectively managed fear. These individuals have demonstrated the ability to confront and overcome their fears, utilizing a combination of emotional intelligence, strategic planning, and resilience. By delving into the experiences of these entrepreneurs, we gain valuable insights into the mindset and strategies required to navigate the uncertainties and challenges of the business world. For example, individuals like Elon Musk and Sara Blakely have faced numerous obstacles and setbacks on their entrepreneurial journeys, yet they have persevered by mastering their fears and leveraging them as motivation for success. These case studies serve as powerful reminders of the transformative power of confronting fear head-on, ultimately leading to personal growth and the achievement of extraordinary accomplishments. Ultimately, by studying these successful entrepreneurs, we can learn valuable lessons in overcoming fear and unlocking our full potential in pursuit of our goals.

XXXI. Fear and Innovation

An essential aspect of human survival lies in the delicate balance between fear and innovation. While fear is a primal instinct that has evolved to protect us from potential threats, harnessing this emotion allows for forward progress and development. Through the lens of reason and modern technology, individuals can transcend their instinctual fears and push the boundaries of what is possible. This duality compels us to confront our fears head-on, using them as a catalyst for growth and advancement. By mastering our innate fears, we can cultivate resilience and self-awareness, fostering a mindset that embraces challenges and thrives in the face of adversity. Fear, when understood and managed effectively, becomes a powerful tool in shaping not just our survival, but also our capacity for innovation and progress in an ever-changing world.

Fear as a barrier to innovation

Throughout history, fear has played a crucial role in human survival, acting as a powerful instinct that warns us of potential dangers. However, fear can also act as a significant barrier to innovation. When individuals are paralyzed by fear, they may be reluctant to try new things, take risks, or push beyond their comfort zones. This reluctance can impede progress and hinder the development of new ideas and technologies. In order to foster innovation, it is essential to address and manage fear effectively. By cultivating a mindset of curiosity, openness, and resilience, individuals can learn to navigate fear and embrace the unknown. Through the practice of facing fears head-on, stepping outside of one's comfort zone, and embracing failure as a learning opportunity, individuals can begin to unlock their creative potential and drive innovation forward. Ultimately, by acknowledging and overcoming fear, individuals can pave the way for new discoveries and groundbreaking advancements in various fields.

Overcoming fear to foster innovation

In the quest for innovation, overcoming fear is a critical challenge that individuals must confront. Fear, although necessary for survival, can also act as a barrier to creativity and progress. By acknowledging and managing our fears, we can break free from the limitations they impose and open ourselves up to new possibilities. By fostering a mindset of courage and resilience, individuals can push past their comfort zones and explore uncharted territories. This willingness to confront fear head-on is essential for fostering innovation, as it enables individuals to take risks, experiment, and think outside the box. Embracing uncertainty and discomfort can lead to breakthroughs and new discoveries. In order to truly innovate, individuals must be willing to face their fears, push through obstacles, and persevere in the face of uncertainty. By doing so, they can unlock their full potential and pave the way for groundbreaking advancements.

Examples of fear-driven innovation

Fear-driven innovation can be seen in various contexts throughout history, showcasing humanity's ability to adapt and thrive in the face of danger. For example, during World War II, the fear of aerial bombardment led to the development of radar technology, revolutionizing modern warfare and civilian safety measures. This fear of mass destruction prompted scientists and engineers to work tirelessly to create innovative solutions to protect populations. Similarly, the fear of pandemics and infectious diseases has spurred advancements in healthcare, leading to the development of vaccines, antibiotics, and improved sanitation practices. These examples demonstrate how fear, when channeled effectively, can drive progress and innovation for the betterment of society. By acknowledging and understanding our fears, we can harness them as a catalyst for positive change and growth, ultimately shaping a more resilient and adaptive future for humanity.

XXXII. Fear and Environmental Challenges

Through the lens of fear and environmental challenges, it becomes evident that our innate survival instinct has a pivotal role in addressing urgent issues such as climate change and resource depletion. Fear can serve as a powerful motivator, prompting individuals and societies to take proactive measures to mitigate environmental threats. By harnessing the fear of irreversible damage to the planet, we can drive collective action towards sustainable practices and conservation efforts. However, fear can also paralyze us, hindering progress and innovation in the face of daunting environmental challenges. Therefore, it is crucial to strike a balance between acknowledging the gravity of the situation and maintaining a sense of optimism and agency. By reframing fear as a catalyst for change rather than a barrier to action, we can mobilize a global response to safeguard the planet for future generations. In this way, fear can be a potent force for positive transformation in the realm of environmental sustainability.

Fear of environmental catastrophes

In the intricate web of human survival, the fear of environmental catastrophes looms as a potent force that triggers our instinctual responses for protection. As we navigate a world fraught with climate change, natural disasters, and pollution, the specter of environmental devastation can evoke a deep-seated fear that threatens our very existence. This fear is not unfounded, as the consequences of environmental degradation are increasingly apparent in our daily lives, from rising sea levels to extreme weather events. The fear of these catastrophes can serve as a powerful motivator for action, driving individuals and communities to advocate for sustainable practices and policies that mitigate ecological harm. Yet, this fear can also lead to feelings of helplessness and despair, paralyzing us in the face of overwhelming environmental challenges. As we grapple with the complexities of our relationship with the environment, confronting our fears head-on and channeling them into positive, proactive change becomes essential for not only our survival but the survival of our planet as well.

Role of fear in promoting environmental action

Having established fear as a fundamental aspect of human biology and survival instincts, it becomes evident that fear can play a crucial role in promoting environmental action. Fear of the consequences of environmental degradation can motivate individuals to take action to protect the planet and ensure a sustainable future. When individuals are confronted with the alarming data on climate change, deforestation, species extinction, and other environmental crises, fear can serve as a powerful catalyst for change. This fear can prompt individuals to adopt more sustainable lifestyle choices, advocate for policy changes, support green initiatives, and participate in grassroots movements aimed at preserving the environment. By tapping into this primal emotion and channeling it towards positive action, fear can be harnessed as a force for environmental activism and collective responsibility in the fight against climate change and ecological destruction. Ultimately, fear can inspire individuals to take meaningful steps towards protecting the planet for future generations.

Managing fear in the context of environmental uncertainty

The ability to manage fear in the face of environmental uncertainty is a crucial skill for human survival. While fear is a natural response designed to protect us from danger, it can also hinder our ability to think clearly and make rational decisions. By learning to master our fear through reason and modern technology, we can navigate challenging situations with calm and composure. Trained individuals, such as firefighters and soldiers, demonstrate how fear can be controlled in extreme circumstances, allowing them to perform effectively under pressure. Through psychological and physical techniques, anyone can improve their capacity to remain calm and clear-headed in high-stress situations. By confronting fears gradually and systematically, we can overcome them and cultivate greater resilience. Ultimately, mastering fear not only enhances our chances of physical survival but also enriches our quality of life by fostering self-awareness and inner strength.

XXXIII. Fear and Global Health

In exploring the intricacies of fear and its role in global health, it becomes evident that this primal instinct can both safeguard and hinder human survival. As individuals, we are biologically hardwired to respond to threats with fear, a mechanism that has served us well throughout evolution. However, in the context of a global health crisis, such as a pandemic, fear can become a double-edged sword. On one hand, fear can motivate individuals to take necessary precautions to protect themselves and others, such as following public health guidelines and seeking medical attention when needed. On the other hand, excessive fear can lead to panic, misinformation, and stigmatization, all of which can impede effective public health responses. Therefore, it is crucial to strike a balance between acknowledging the legitimate concerns that fear may provoke and preventing it from spiraling out of control. By fostering a climate of education, empathy, and evidence-based decision-making, society can harness the power of fear to promote global health and well-being.

Fear during global health crises

In the realm of global health crises, fear often becomes a prevailing force that shapes individual and collective responses. When faced with uncertainty and potential threats to one's well-being, fear can spread rapidly and lead to panic, irrational behavior, and even social unrest. As seen in recent pandemics or outbreaks, the fear of an invisible enemy can grip populations, causing them to stockpile resources, avoid necessary medical care, and distrust authorities. This fear during global health crises is not unfounded, as the stakes are high, and the consequences can be severe. However, it is essential to recognize that fear, if not managed properly, can exacerbate the situation and hinder effective responses. Therefore, it is crucial to strike a balance between acknowledging the legitimate concerns that fuel fear and maintaining a sense of rationality and calmness in order to navigate through turbulent times with clarity and resilience.

Managing public fear in pandemics

Fear in pandemics poses a significant challenge for public health authorities, as managing this emotion can greatly impact the effectiveness of response strategies. During outbreaks of infectious diseases, such as the recent COVID-19 pandemic, fear can spread as rapidly as the virus itself, leading to panic, misinformation, and noncompliance with public health measures. Therefore, it is crucial for authorities to find ways to address and manage public fear in order to maintain trust, cooperation, and adherence to recommended guidelines. By providing clear and transparent communication, accurate information, and demonstrating empathy towards the public's concerns, authorities can help alleviate fears and promote a sense of control and safety. Additionally, implementing measures to ensure the availability of resources, such as medical supplies and support services, can help mitigate fear and uncertainty, ultimately enhancing the overall response to pandemics. By effectively managing public fear, authorities can not only contain the spread of the disease but also foster resilience and unity within the community.

Lessons learned from managing fear in global health emergencies

In the context of global health emergencies, the management of fear plays a crucial role in shaping the response and outcome of such crises. Lessons learned from previous outbreaks, such as the Ebola virus or the COVID-19 pandemic, have underscored the significance of effectively managing fear to ensure the implementation of necessary public health measures and to prevent panic among the population. By understanding the psychological aspects of fear in emergency situations, healthcare professionals and policymakers can develop strategies to address fear-induced behaviors and misinformation that may hinder the control of the outbreak. Utilizing methods such as communication campaigns, mental health support for frontline workers, and transparent information sharing can help build trust and alleviate anxiety within communities facing health emergencies. Ultimately, mastering fear in global health crises is not only essential for containing the spread of diseases but also for safeguarding public health and well-being.

XXXIV. Fear and Aging

As individuals age, the relationship between fear and aging becomes increasingly evident. Older adults often face a multitude of fears, ranging from the fear of physical decline and illness to the fear of social isolation and loss of independence. These fears can be exacerbated by the natural process of aging, as well as by external factors such as societal attitudes towards aging. Moreover, the accumulation of life experiences can contribute to the development of new fears or the amplification of existing ones. However, it is essential to recognize that fear is a natural response to the challenges and uncertainties that come with aging. By acknowledging and understanding these fears, individuals can proactively address them through strategies such as seeking social support, maintaining a healthy lifestyle, and engaging in activities that promote mental and emotional well-being. Ultimately, by confronting and managing their fears, older adults can navigate the aging process with resilience and grace.

Common fears about aging

Fear of aging is a common and universal concern that many individuals face as they grow older. The apprehension of physical decline, the loss of independence, and the fear of being a burden on loved ones can be overwhelming. This fear is often fueled by societal pressures to maintain a youthful appearance and productivity, leading to feelings of inadequacy and insecurity. Moreover, the prospect of facing one's mortality can evoke existential dread and anxiety about the unknown. Despite these fears, aging is a natural and inevitable part of life that should be embraced rather than avoided. By reframing our perspective on aging and focusing on the wisdom and experiences gained with age, we can overcome these fears and approach the aging process with grace and acceptance. It is essential to cultivate a positive outlook on aging, recognizing that it is a privilege denied to many and an opportunity for personal growth and self-discovery. Ultimately, by confronting and acknowledging our fears about aging, we can navigate the challenges of growing older with resilience and dignity.

Managing fear in the elderly

Fear, particularly in the elderly population, can be a complex emotion to manage. As individuals age, they may face a myriad of fears ranging from health concerns to social isolation. It is crucial to acknowledge and address these fears in order to ensure the well-being and quality of life for the elderly. Techniques such as cognitive-behavioral therapy and mindfulness practices can be effective in helping seniors identify and cope with their fears in a constructive manner. By encouraging open communication and providing a supportive environment, caregivers and healthcare professionals can assist the elderly in navigating their fears and anxieties. Additionally, engaging in activities that promote physical and mental well-being, such as exercise and social interactions, can help mitigate the effects of fear in older individuals. Ultimately, managing fear in the elderly requires a holistic approach that considers their unique needs and challenges in order to promote a sense of security and peace of mind.

Strategies to reduce fear-related stress in aging populations

Taking into consideration the specific challenges faced by aging populations in managing fear-related stress, there are several strategies that can be implemented to help alleviate this burden. One effective approach is implementing mindfulness and relaxation techniques, which have shown promising results in reducing anxiety and fear in older adults. These practices not only help individuals to stay present and focused but also promote a sense of calm and inner peace. Additionally, engaging in regular physical activity has been proven to be beneficial in reducing stress and anxiety levels, as exercise releases endorphins that can improve mood and overall well-being. Social support networks are another crucial factor in mitigating fear-related stress in aging populations, as having a strong support system can provide comfort, encouragement, and a sense of belonging. By incorporating these strategies into the lives of older individuals, it is possible to significantly reduce fear-related stress and enhance their overall quality of life.

XXXV. Fear and Gender

Fear is a universal emotion that transcends boundaries of gender, yet its manifestations can be influenced by societal constructs and expectations. Traditional gender roles often dictate that men should be stoic and fearless, while women are allowed to express more vulnerability and fear. This dichotomy can result in men feeling pressured to suppress their fears, leading to potential mental health issues. On the other hand, women may be perceived as weak or overly emotional if they exhibit fear, which can undermine their confidence and agency. It is crucial to recognize that fear is a natural response to danger, regardless of gender, and should not be stigmatized or dismissed based on societal norms. By understanding and addressing these gendered perceptions of fear, individuals can begin to create a more inclusive and supportive environment where all individuals, regardless of gender, can feel empowered to acknowledge and confront their fears in a healthy and constructive manner.

Gender differences in fear responses

Fear responses can vary between genders due to a combination of biological, psychological, and sociocultural factors. Research indicates that women tend to experience fear more intensely and exhibit higher levels of anxiety compared to men. Evolutionary theories suggest that this difference may stem from the need for women to protect themselves and their offspring from potential threats, leading to a heightened sensitivity to danger. Additionally, societal norms and expectations can influence how men and women express fear, with women often being socialized to be more emotionally expressive and open about their fears. On the other hand, men may feel pressure to appear stoic and fearless, which can impact how they acknowledge and address their own fears. Understanding and acknowledging these gender differences in fear responses is essential for developing more effective strategies for managing fear and promoting mental well-being in both men and women. By recognizing and addressing these differences, individuals can cultivate a healthier relationship with fear and work towards mastering their responses for improved overall resilience and coping mechanisms.

Social constructions of fear and gender

Understanding the social constructions of fear and gender sheds light on how individuals navigate and interpret their experiences in society. Fear, often portrayed as a sign of weakness, is sometimes gendered in ways that reinforce traditional stereotypes. Men are expected to exhibit courage and dominance, while women are often encouraged to be more nurturing and passive. These societal expectations can influence how individuals perceive and express their fears, shaping their sense of identity and behavior. For instance, women may be more likely to internalize their fears due to the pressure to appear strong, while men may feel less comfortable seeking help for anxiety or vulnerability. By exploring how fear and gender intersect in social contexts, we can challenge these stereotypes and create a more inclusive and empathetic society where individuals are free to express and process their fears without judgment. Ultimately, breaking down these constructs allows for a deeper understanding of the complex interplay between fear, gender, and social dynamics.

Addressing gender-specific fears

Gender-specific fears can be deeply ingrained in individuals due to societal norms and expectations. Women, in particular, may fear situations such as walking alone at night or being sexually harassed, whereas men may have fears surrounding failure or weakness. These gender-specific fears can be detrimental to individuals' mental health and overall well-being if left unaddressed. It is essential to acknowledge and confront these fears in order to break free from their constraints and live more authentically. By recognizing and challenging these fears, individuals can empower themselves to overcome societal expectations and norms that contribute to their anxieties. Through introspection and self-awareness, individuals can begin to dismantle these fears and reclaim their agency. It is crucial to create safe spaces for individuals to address these gender-specific fears openly and support one another in the process of liberation and personal growth. In doing so, we can cultivate a more inclusive and understanding society that fosters resilience and empowerment for all.

XXXVI. Fear and Race

In examining the intersection of fear and race, it becomes evident that historical and societal factors have deeply entrenched fear within racial dynamics. The history of racial discrimination and violence has perpetuated a climate where fear often accompanies interactions between individuals of different races. This fear is not innate but rather cultivated through generations of prejudice and oppression. Studies have shown that individuals from marginalized racial groups often experience heightened levels of fear and anxiety due to the systemic racism they face daily. This fear can manifest in various forms, including fear of discrimination, violence, or being misunderstood. Furthermore, the fear experienced by marginalized racial groups is often dismissed or ignored, further exacerbating the divide between races. To address this issue, it is crucial to acknowledge and actively work towards dismantling the structures that perpetuate fear based on race, promoting empathy, understanding, and equality among all individuals, regardless of their racial background. By confronting and dismantling these fears, society can move towards a more inclusive and just future.

Racial disparities in fear and anxiety

The impact of racial disparities on levels of fear and anxiety is a critical issue that cannot be overlooked. Research has shown that individuals from marginalized racial groups often experience higher levels of fear and anxiety due to systemic discrimination, historical trauma, and social inequality. This heightened sense of fear can have detrimental effects on both mental and physical health, leading to increased stress, chronic illnesses, and decreased quality of life. Moreover, the fear and anxiety experienced by individuals from these groups can be further amplified by media portrayals, stereotypes, and microaggressions. It is crucial for society to acknowledge and address these racial disparities in fear and anxiety in order to promote equity, social justice, and overall well-being for all individuals. By recognizing and working to eliminate these disparities, we can create a more inclusive and supportive environment where individuals of all races can thrive and feel safe.

Historical context of fear and race relations

The historical context of fear and race relations is a complex and tumultuous one, shaped by centuries of power dynamics, oppression, and social constructs. Fear has been used as a tool to control and manipulate marginalized groups, instilling a sense of inferiority and subjugation. From slavery in the United States to apartheid in South Africa, fear has been weaponized to maintain systems of racial hierarchy and privilege. The fear of the 'other,' fueled by ignorance and prejudice, has perpetuated cycles of violence and discrimination throughout history. However, there have also been moments of resistance and resilience in the face of fear, where individuals and communities have come together to challenge oppressive systems and demand justice and equality. By understanding the historical roots of fear and race relations, we can better navigate the complexities of our present society and work towards building a more equitable and inclusive future for all.

Strategies for addressing racially induced fears

In addressing racially induced fears, individuals and societies must employ a multifaceted approach that combines education, communication, and empathy. By promoting understanding and knowledge of different cultures and backgrounds, stereotypes and misconceptions can be dismantled, leading to a more inclusive and harmonious society. Encouraging open dialogue and meaningful discussions about racial issues can help bridge the gap between communities and foster a sense of unity. Additionally, cultivating empathy and compassion towards others can help individuals recognize and challenge their own biases, promoting a more empathetic and tolerant society. By implementing these strategies at both the individual and societal levels, racially induced fears can be addressed effectively, ultimately leading to a more peaceful and equitable coexistence among diverse groups.

XXXVII. Fear and Disability

As fear is deeply embedded in our biological makeup, it is crucial to recognize its impact on individuals with disabilities. Fear and disability can exacerbate the challenges faced by those already dealing with physical or cognitive impairments. The fear of the unknown, of being unable to navigate the world as freely as others, can create a heightened sense of vulnerability for individuals with disabilities. This fear may manifest in anxiety, depression, or even avoidance behavior that further limits their opportunities for growth and independence. It is essential for society to address these fears through increased awareness, support systems, and accessibility measures that empower individuals with disabilities to face their fears with confidence. By acknowledging and addressing the unique intersection of fear and disability, we can work towards a more inclusive and supportive environment for those who may already be struggling with additional obstacles in their daily lives.

Unique fears faced by individuals with disabilities

In the realm of fear and survival, individuals with disabilities face unique challenges that set them apart from the general population. These individuals often have to navigate a world that is not always accommodating to their needs, leading to fears related to accessibility, discrimination, and independence. The fear of being unable to access essential services or navigate public spaces can be a constant source of anxiety for those with physical disabilities. Additionally, there is the fear of facing discrimination or prejudice, whether in employment, education, or social interactions. Furthermore, the fear of losing independence and relying heavily on others for basic needs can be overwhelming for individuals with disabilities. These fears not only impact their daily lives but also have a profound effect on their mental and emotional well-being. It is crucial to acknowledge and address these unique fears faced by individuals with disabilities in order to create a more inclusive and supportive society for all.

Overcoming fear-related barriers for the disabled

Through a combination of education, awareness, and accessibility, fear-related barriers for disabled individuals can be effectively overcome. By providing support systems that cater to the specific needs of the disabled population, such as specialized training programs and adaptive technology, individuals can learn to navigate their fears and challenges with confidence. Moreover, fostering a culture of inclusivity and understanding within society can help reduce the stigma and discrimination that often exacerbate fear in disabled individuals. By empowering them with the tools and resources they need to thrive, we can create a more equitable and supportive environment for all. Ultimately, by addressing fear-related barriers head-on and advocating for the rights of the disabled community, we can work towards a more inclusive and compassionate society where fear no longer hinders the opportunities and potential of individuals with disabilities.

Inclusive strategies to manage fear in disabled populations

When addressing the management of fear in disabled populations, inclusive strategies must be considered to ensure that individuals with disabilities have equal access to techniques that can help them cope with their fears. One such strategy is the development of tailored programs that take into account the specific needs and challenges faced by disabled individuals, whether they be physical, cognitive, or emotional. By providing personalized support and accommodations, such as using alternative communication methods for those with speech impairments or creating sensory-friendly environments for those with sensory sensitivities, fear management programs can be more effective and accessible for all. Additionally, promoting a culture of inclusivity and understanding within these programs can help empower disabled individuals to confront their fears in a safe and supportive environment. Overall, by implementing inclusive strategies, fear management programs can better serve the diverse needs of disabled populations, ultimately leading to improved overall well-being and quality of life.

XXXVIII. Fear and Trauma

In exploring the intricate interplay between fear and trauma, it becomes evident that these primal responses are deeply interconnected within the human psyche. Fear, as a fundamental survival mechanism, triggers our fight-or-flight response when faced with danger, while trauma can result from overwhelming experiences that leave lasting psychological scars. While fear may serve to protect us from immediate threats, unchecked or unresolved trauma can lead to debilitating anxiety and other mental health issues. The effects of fear and trauma can be insidious, infiltrating every aspect of our lives and limiting our potential for growth and fulfillment. It is crucial to recognize the impact of these emotions and work towards developing healthy coping mechanisms to navigate life's challenges effectively. By addressing our fears head-on and seeking professional help when trauma arises, we can take proactive steps towards healing and resilience, ultimately reclaiming our power over these primal instincts.

Relationship between fear and trauma

In the intricate web of human survival, the relationship between fear and trauma serves as a crucial intersection of instinct and reason. Fear, deeply rooted in our evolutionary history, acts as a protective mechanism, alerting us to potential dangers and triggering the necessary physiological responses for survival. However, when fear becomes overwhelming and uncontrollable, it can lead to trauma, leaving deep emotional scars that hinder one's ability to function effectively. The key lies in mastering fear through reason and understanding, allowing individuals to confront and process their fears in a healthy manner. Whether it is through gradual exposure therapy or cognitive-behavioral techniques, learning to navigate the intricate dance between fear and trauma is essential for overcoming psychological barriers and enhancing resilience. By fostering a mindset that views fear not as an enemy to be avoided but as a guiding force that can be harnessed, individuals can embrace their fears, conquer trauma, and ultimately thrive in the face of adversity.

Therapeutic approaches to fear stemming from trauma

In confronting fear stemming from trauma, therapeutic approaches play a pivotal role in facilitating healing and promoting resilience. By employing evidence-based interventions such as cognitive-behavioral therapy (CBT) or eye movement desensitization and reprocessing (EMDR), individuals can address the root causes of their fear responses and work towards resolving underlying traumas. These therapeutic practices provide a structured framework for processing and making sense of past experiences, allowing individuals to gradually confront their fears in a safe and controlled environment. Additionally, mindfulness-based techniques have been shown to be effective in managing fear and stress, helping individuals develop a greater sense of awareness and acceptance of their emotions. By combining these approaches with a supportive therapeutic relationship, individuals can begin to reframe their perceptions of fear, ultimately empowering them to move beyond trauma and towards a place of healing and growth.

Case studies of overcoming trauma-related fears

The case studies of individuals who have successfully overcome trauma-related fears provide valuable insight into the power of resilience and determination in the face of adversity. These real-life examples showcase the potential for growth and healing even in the most challenging of circumstances. By examining how these individuals have confronted their fears head-on and worked diligently to regain control over their emotions, we can learn valuable lessons about the human capacity for transformation and recovery. Through methods such as exposure therapy, cognitive-behavioral techniques, and support from mental health professionals, these individuals have been able to reclaim their lives from the grip of trauma and fear. These case studies serve as a beacon of hope for anyone struggling with similar issues, demonstrating that with the right tools and support, it is possible to overcome even the most deeply ingrained fears. By studying these success stories, we can gain a deeper understanding of the resilience of the human spirit and the potential for growth and healing in the face of trauma.

XXXIX. Fear and Therapy

Fear, as a primal instinct deeply ingrained in our biological makeup, serves as a crucial mechanism for human survival. It is a response that has evolved over millennia to protect us from potential threats, triggering a fight-or-flight response that can be life-saving in dangerous situations. However, the ability to manage and control fear is equally essential for survival, especially in extreme circumstances where clear and rational thinking is paramount. Trained professionals such as firefighters and soldiers exemplify how fear can be harnessed and regulated to perform effectively under pressure. Psychological and physical techniques exist to empower individuals to confront and overcome their fears, ultimately leading to increased self-awareness and resilience. By viewing fear not as an adversary, but rather as a powerful ally that can be understood and mastered, we can cultivate a greater sense of calm, clarity, and personal growth in the face of adversity.

Psychological therapies for managing fear

The utilization of psychological therapies in managing fear is vital for enhancing individuals' ability to navigate high-stress situations effectively. By delving into the realm of cognitive-behavioral interventions, individuals can learn to reframe their thoughts and responses to fear triggers, ultimately empowering themselves to confront and overcome their fears. Techniques such as exposure therapy and mindfulness meditation offer practical tools to desensitize individuals to their fears gradually, allowing for a controlled and systematic approach to fear management. Through these therapies, individuals can develop a deeper understanding of their fear responses and cultivate the resilience needed to face their fears head-on. By acknowledging fear as a natural and adaptive response, individuals can harness its energy to propel them forward rather than hinder their progress. In mastering fear through psychological interventions, individuals can not only enhance their survival instincts, but also improve their overall well-being and quality of life.

Role of cognitive-behavioral therapy in fear reduction

In addressing fear reduction, cognitive-behavioral therapy (CBT) plays a crucial role in helping individuals manage and overcome their anxieties. By focusing on identifying and changing negative thought patterns and behaviors, CBT offers practical techniques to challenge irrational fears and replace them with more rational responses. This form of therapy empowers individuals to confront their fears head-on, rather than avoiding them, which can ultimately lead to greater resilience and self-confidence. Through a systematic approach that combines cognitive restructuring and exposure therapy, CBT helps individuals gradually desensitize themselves to the source of their fear, enabling them to regain control over their emotions and reactions. Research shows that CBT can be highly effective in treating various anxiety disorders, phobias, and post-traumatic stress disorder, highlighting its efficacy in fear reduction. By equipping individuals with the tools to reframe their thinking and confront their fears, CBT serves as a valuable resource in helping individuals navigate the complex terrain of fear and anxiety.

Innovative therapeutic techniques for fear management

When faced with debilitating fear, individuals are increasingly turning to innovative therapeutic techniques for fear management. These cutting-edge methods offer a new approach to addressing deep-rooted fears and phobias by integrating technology and psychology. Virtual reality exposure therapy, for example, allows individuals to gradually confront their fears in a safe and controlled environment, helping them desensitize and reframe their reactions. Similarly, biofeedback techniques enable individuals to regulate physiological responses to fear-inducing stimuli, empowering them to take control over their bodily reactions. By combining traditional psychological interventions with technological advancements, these innovative therapeutic techniques provide a holistic approach to fear management that can be tailored to individual needs and preferences. As advancements in the field of psychology continue to evolve, these techniques offer promising solutions for effectively managing and overcoming fears, ultimately promoting improved mental well-being and quality of life.

XL. Fear and Pharmaceuticals

Throughout history, fear has played a crucial role in the survival of our species, acting as a powerful motivator to avoid danger and threats. As humans evolved, our ability to understand and manage fear became more sophisticated, leading to the development of pharmaceuticals to help alleviate symptoms of anxiety and fear-related disorders. While medications can be useful in certain situations to mitigate extreme fear responses, there is a growing concern that over-reliance on pharmaceuticals may hinder our natural ability to confront and overcome fears. It is essential to strike a balance between utilizing modern treatments and relying on our innate resilience and coping mechanisms. By combining pharmaceutical interventions with cognitive-behavioral therapies and mindfulness practices, individuals can effectively manage their fears without becoming dependent on medications. This integrated approach ensures that fear is not simply suppressed but understood and conquered, empowering individuals to navigate challenging situations with resilience and self-awareness.

Medications used in the treatment of fear-related disorders

The treatment of fear-related disorders often involves the use of medications to help manage symptoms and provide relief for individuals suffering from conditions such as anxiety, panic attacks, or PTSD. Medications such as selective serotonin reuptake inhibitors (SSRIs) and benzodiazepines are commonly prescribed to address the underlying chemical imbalances that contribute to these disorders. SSRIs work by increasing the levels of serotonin in the brain, which can help regulate mood and reduce feelings of anxiety. On the other hand, benzodiazepines act as sedatives, calming the nervous system and alleviating symptoms of acute anxiety or panic. While these medications can be effective in the short term, it is important to use them in conjunction with therapy and other interventions to address the root causes of fear-related disorders. Additionally, careful monitoring and management of medication use are essential to avoid potential side effects and dependencies that can arise from long-term use. By incorporating medications as part of a comprehensive treatment plan, individuals can better manage their fear-related disorders and improve their overall quality of life.

Pros and cons of pharmacological interventions for fear

In exploring the pros and cons of pharmacological interventions for fear, it is essential to consider the potential benefits and drawbacks of such treatments. On one hand, medications can provide quick relief for individuals suffering from debilitating anxiety or phobias, allowing them to function more effectively in their daily lives. Drugs like benzodiazepines can offer immediate relief from acute episodes of fear, offering a sense of calm and control in stressful situations. However, the use of pharmacological interventions can also come with risks and side effects that need to be carefully considered. Addiction, dependency, and the potential for negative interactions with other medications are all important factors to weigh when deciding on a treatment plan. While medication can be a valuable tool in managing fear, it should be utilized judiciously and in conjunction with other therapeutic approaches to ensure holistic and sustainable outcomes.

Future directions in fear-targeting pharmaceuticals

An intriguing area for future exploration in fear-targeting pharmaceuticals lies in the development of precision medications that can target specific fear-related neural circuits in the brain. By dissecting the intricate pathways involved in fear responses, researchers can potentially design drugs that modulate these circuits without impeding other cognitive functions. This approach could revolutionize the treatment of anxiety disorders by providing more targeted and effective interventions with fewer side effects. Furthermore, advancements in biomarker research may lead to the identification of individualized fear signatures, allowing for personalized pharmacological treatments tailored to each person's unique neural makeup. As we delve deeper into the intersection of neuroscience and pharmacology, the potential for unlocking new avenues in fear modulation becomes increasingly promising, offering hope for more efficient and nuanced approaches to managing fear-related pathologies in the future.

XLI. Fear and Alternative Medicine

Through the lens of fear and alternative medicine, it becomes apparent how our instinctual responses to perceived threats have shaped our approach to healthcare. Alternative medicine, often viewed with skepticism in conventional circles, can be seen as a manifestation of our fear of traditional medical treatments. The fear of side effects, invasive procedures, or the unknown drives individuals to seek out alternative treatments that promise a gentler approach. However, this fear-driven decision-making process can sometimes lead to the dismissal of evidence-based medicine in favor of unproven or potentially harmful remedies. It is crucial to strike a balance between acknowledging and addressing our fears surrounding conventional medicine while also critically evaluating the efficacy and safety of alternative treatments. By approaching alternative medicine with a discerning eye and an open mind, individuals can make informed decisions that prioritize both their health and well-being. Fear should not dictate our choices in healthcare but instead serve as a motivation to seek out the most effective and evidence-based treatments available.

Role of alternative medicine in managing fear

In the realm of managing fear, alternative medicine plays a crucial role in providing individuals with holistic approaches to address their anxieties. While traditional medicine often focuses on treating symptoms, alternative medicine delves into the root causes of fear and offers a range of therapies that aim to balance the mind, body, and spirit. Practices such as acupuncture, meditation, yoga, and herbal remedies have been shown to reduce stress levels, promote relaxation, and cultivate a sense of inner peace. By incorporating alternative medicine into their fear-management strategies, individuals can tap into a more comprehensive toolkit for addressing their emotional well-being. These approaches not only provide relief from immediate fears but also offer long-term benefits by fostering resilience, emotional stability, and a deeper sense of self-awareness. As such, alternative medicine serves as a valuable ally in the journey towards mastering fear and achieving a more balanced and harmonious state of being.

Techniques such as meditation and acupuncture for fear reduction

Throughout history, humans have utilized a variety of techniques to reduce fear and manage stress in high-pressure situations. One such method is meditation, a practice that has been scientifically proven to reduce anxiety and promote a sense of inner peace. By focusing on breathing and mindfulness, individuals can train their minds to remain calm in the face of fear. Acupuncture, on the other hand, is an ancient Chinese therapy that involves inserting needles into specific points on the body to balance energy flow and alleviate stress. This technique has shown promise in reducing fear and anxiety by promoting relaxation and releasing endorphins. By incorporating these techniques into daily routines, individuals can develop a proactive approach to fear reduction, enhancing their ability to remain clear-headed and composed in challenging situations. Overall, meditation and acupuncture offer effective tools for mastering fear and achieving a greater sense of self-control and resilience.

Effectiveness of alternative treatments in fear management

In the exploration of fear management, it becomes evident that alternative treatments can indeed play a significant role in effectively controlling this powerful emotion. While traditional methods like medication or therapy are common, alternative approaches such as mindfulness, meditation, acupuncture, or even virtual reality exposure therapy have shown promise in helping individuals confront and conquer their fears. These alternative treatments often focus on addressing the underlying emotions and psychological factors contributing to fear, offering a more holistic approach to fear management. Moreover, they can provide individuals with practical tools and techniques to cope with fear in real-time, enabling them to face their anxieties head-on and gradually build resilience. By combining traditional methods with alternative treatments, individuals can develop a comprehensive fear management plan tailored to their unique needs and circumstances, ultimately leading to a more balanced and empowered approach to overcoming fear.

XLII. Fear and Physical Health

In understanding the intricate connection between fear and physical health, it becomes evident that our biological responses to threats have been finely tuned through evolution for our survival. Fear, as a primal instinct, triggers a cascade of physiological reactions designed to prepare the body for fight or flight. However, in modern-day society, where constant stressors can perpetuate a state of chronic fear, it is imperative to learn how to master this innate response. By examining how trained individuals, such as firefighters and soldiers, can effectively manage their fear in high-pressure situations, we can glean insights into methods to improve our own fear response. Techniques like gradual exposure and systematic desensitization provide structured approaches to confront and overcome fears, ultimately leading to enhanced resilience and improved physical well-being. In mastering fear, not as an enemy but as an ally, we can unlock the potential for greater self-awareness and a higher quality of life.

Physical health consequences of prolonged fear

Fear, if left unaddressed and prolonged, can have significant physical health consequences on the body. Chronic fear triggers the release of stress hormones, such as cortisol and adrenaline, which can lead to high blood pressure, weakened immune function, and increased risk of heart disease. The prolonged activation of the body's stress response system can result in inflammation, muscle tension, and digestive issues, all of which can contribute to long-term health problems. Additionally, constant fear and anxiety can negatively impact sleep patterns, leading to sleep disturbances and insomnia, further exacerbating the toll on physical health. A study by the University of California, Berkeley, found that individuals who experienced chronic fear and anxiety had a higher risk of developing chronic health conditions over time. Therefore, it is essential to address and manage fear effectively to protect not only mental well-being but also physical health in the long run. By learning to confront fears and cultivate resilience, individuals can minimize the detrimental effects of prolonged fear on their overall well-being.

Fear's impact on the immune system

Fear's impact on the immune system is a topic of significant interest in the fields of psychology and medicine. Research has shown that chronic stress and fear can weaken the immune system, making individuals more susceptible to illness and disease. When the body is in a constant state of fear, the production of cortisol, known as the stress hormone, increases significantly, which can suppress the immune system's ability to fight off infections. This can lead to a higher risk of developing chronic conditions such as heart disease, diabetes, and autoimmune disorders. Additionally, fear can have a detrimental effect on overall well-being, as heightened levels of anxiety and worry can contribute to inflammation in the body, further compromising the immune response. Therefore, it is essential to address and manage fear effectively in order to maintain a healthy immune system and overall physical health.

Strategies to mitigate physical health impacts of fear

In order to mitigate the physical health impacts of fear, individuals can employ various strategies that focus on both the mind and body. One effective approach is practicing mindfulness and relaxation techniques to remain calm and centered in the face of fear-inducing situations. By learning to control their physiological responses through deep breathing exercises and visualization, individuals can reduce the physical manifestations of fear such as increased heart rate and tense muscles. Additionally, engaging in regular physical exercise can help to improve overall physical health and resilience, making it easier to cope with stress and fear. Furthermore, seeking professional help from therapists or counselors can provide valuable tools and coping mechanisms for managing fear and its effects on the body. By combining these strategies with a strong support system and a proactive mindset, individuals can effectively mitigate the physical health impacts of fear and enhance their overall well-being.

XLIII. Fear and Mental Health

In the realm of mental health, fear plays a pivotal role that cannot be ignored. While fear is often seen as a hindrance, it can actually serve as a beacon shining light on underlying issues that require attention. This emotional response can alert individuals to danger or potential harm, prompting them to take necessary precautions to ensure their safety. However, when fear becomes overwhelming or irrational, it can lead to debilitating anxiety and other mental health challenges. The key lies in striking a balance between acknowledging the validity of one's fears and not allowing them to dictate one's actions or emotions. By developing coping mechanisms and seeking professional help when needed, individuals can navigate the complex landscape of fear and mental health with resilience and grace. Embracing fear as a part of the human experience, rather than avoiding or suppressing it, can lead to profound growth and self-awareness in the journey towards optimal mental well-being.

Mental health disorders associated with excessive fear

In considering mental health disorders associated with excessive fear, it is crucial to understand the complex interplay between our innate survival instincts and the modern challenges of managing overwhelming anxiety. Excessive fear, when left unchecked, can lead to debilitating conditions such as phobias, panic disorders, and post-traumatic stress disorder. These disorders can significantly impact an individual's quality of life, interfering with their ability to function effectively in everyday situations. However, with the right interventions and treatments, individuals can learn to cope with and overcome their excessive fears. Therapy, medication, and cognitive-behavioral techniques can all be effective tools in helping individuals manage their fears and regain a sense of control over their lives. By addressing these mental health disorders associated with excessive fear head-on, individuals can work towards a healthier and more fulfilling life, free from the constraints of irrational anxiety.

Preventative mental health strategies for managing fear

In light of the inherent physiological and psychological responses to fear, it is imperative to explore preventative mental health strategies for managing this primal instinct. While fear may serve as a vital tool for survival, unchecked and irrational fear can lead to detrimental consequences for individuals' well-being. By adopting proactive approaches, individuals can cultivate resilience and emotional regulation skills to effectively navigate fear-inducing situations. Techniques such as mindfulness, cognitive-behavioral therapy, and self-care practices can equip individuals with the tools needed to confront and mitigate fear in a controlled manner. Furthermore, establishing a support network and seeking professional guidance can aid in developing a comprehensive approach to managing fear before it escalates to a debilitating state. Emphasizing the importance of early intervention and ongoing self-awareness, these preventative mental health strategies can empower individuals to harness fear as a mechanism for personal growth and emotional stability, promoting overall well-being and resilience in the face of adversity.

Mental health support systems for fear-related conditions

In the realm of mental health support systems for fear-related conditions, it is essential to recognize the multifaceted nature of fear and its impact on individuals' well-being. Addressing fear-related conditions requires a comprehensive approach that encompasses both psychological and physiological interventions. Therapeutic techniques such as cognitive-behavioral therapy (CBT) have been shown to be effective in helping individuals identify and challenge irrational beliefs and maladaptive behaviors associated with fear. Additionally, mindfulness-based interventions can help individuals develop a greater sense of awareness and acceptance of their emotions, including fear, allowing them to respond to challenging situations more effectively. By integrating these approaches into mental health support systems, individuals can learn to manage their fears in a healthy and adaptive manner, ultimately improving their overall quality of life and well-being. Overall, fostering a greater understanding of fear and implementing evidence-based interventions are critical in providing effective support for individuals struggling with fear-related conditions.

XLIV. Fear and Resilience

As the essay delves into the intricate interplay between fear and resilience, it becomes evident that fear, despite its negative connotations, is a vital instinct deeply rooted in human survival. Our biological makeup predisposes us to respond to threats swiftly and instinctually. However, the real challenge lies in mastering this primal response through reason and technological advancements. Examining how professionals like firefighters and soldiers undergo rigorous training to combat fear in high-pressure situations sheds light on the attainability of fear management. This leads to a discussion on the psychology and physical strategies that can be universally adopted to improve one's composure when faced with adversity. Moreover, the essay emphasizes the significance of repeatedly confronting fears to ultimately conquer them, emphasizing the efficacy of gradual exposure and systematic desensitization. By concluding with a reminder of the transformative power fear can have when understood and controlled, the essay effectively highlights how mastering fear is not just about physical survival but also about enhancing the overall quality of life.

Building resilience to manage fear

In the intricate web of human survival, building resilience to manage fear emerges as a crucial skill that can mean the difference between life and death. While fear is undeniably a deeply ingrained instinct meant to protect us from harm, it can also be a paralyzing force that inhibits rational decision-making. This duality of fear presents a compelling challenge for individuals seeking to navigate perilous situations with composure and clarity. By harnessing the power of reason and modern techniques, individuals can learn to confront and conquer their fears, cultivating a sense of inner strength and fortitude. Through mental and physical exercises, individuals can gradually desensitize themselves to fear, allowing them to develop a resilient mindset that enables them to face adversity with courage and tenacity. Ultimately, by mastering fear, individuals not only enhance their chances of physical survival but also cultivate a deep sense of self-awareness and emotional resilience that enriches their lives beyond measure.

Role of resilience training in overcoming fear

The role of resilience training plays a crucial part in overcoming fear, especially in high-stress situations where a calm and collected response is essential for survival. By undergoing specific training techniques, individuals can learn to control their emotional responses and channel their fear into productive actions. Through practices such as gradual exposure and systematic desensitization, individuals can confront their fears head-on, allowing them to build resilience and reduce the impact of fear on their decision-making processes. Moreover, resilience training can help individuals develop a sense of self-awareness and emotional intelligence, enabling them to navigate challenging situations with confidence and composure. Ultimately, by mastering fear through resilience training, individuals can not only enhance their survival instincts but also improve their overall quality of life by cultivating a mindset of strength and adaptability in the face of adversity.

Examples of resilience overcoming fear in real-life scenarios

In real-life scenarios, examples of resilience overcoming fear can be seen in individuals facing extreme challenges. One compelling instance is that of Aron Ralston, the hiker who became trapped by a boulder in a remote canyon. Despite his initial fear and desperation, Ralston displayed remarkable resilience by rationing his supplies, mustering his physical strength, and ultimately making the difficult decision to amputate his own arm to free himself. This act of courage and determination in the face of overwhelming fear showcases the human capacity to overcome even the most daunting obstacles through sheer willpower and resourcefulness. Ralston's story serves as a powerful reminder that resilience is not the absence of fear, but rather the ability to confront and transcend it in pursuit of survival and success. By harnessing inner strength and pushing past their limits, individuals like Ralston demonstrate the transformative power of resilience in the face of fear.

XLV. Fear and Self-Efficacy

Throughout human history, fear has played a crucial role in our survival instincts. From the early days of our ancestors roaming the savannahs to modern society, fear has been a natural response deeply rooted in our biology. However, as we have evolved and developed more complex societies, the management of fear has become essential. Trained professionals like firefighters and soldiers exemplify how fear can be controlled and even utilized to enhance performance in high-stress situations. By employing psychological and physical techniques, individuals can learn to confront and gradually overcome their fears. This process of desensitization and exposure is key to mastering fear, as it equips us with the resilience needed to face challenges head-on. Ultimately, understanding and managing fear not only improves physical survival but also enhances our quality of life by fostering a sense of self-awareness and inner strength. Fear, when harnessed effectively, can indeed be our greatest ally.

Relationship between self-efficacy and fear

Fear, as a primal instinct deeply ingrained in our biology, serves as a crucial mechanism for human survival. However, the relationship between self-efficacy and fear plays a significant role in determining how individuals respond to threats and challenges. Research indicates that individuals with high levels of self-efficacy are more likely to approach fearful situations with resilience and confidence, viewing obstacles as opportunities for growth rather than insurmountable barriers. This suggests that a strong sense of self-efficacy can serve as a buffer against the debilitating effects of fear, allowing individuals to maintain composure and focus in high-stress environments. By cultivating self-belief and a positive internal dialogue, individuals can effectively manage fear and harness its energy for productive action. Ultimately, the connection between self-efficacy and fear highlights the importance of mindset in shaping our responses to adversity, underscoring the transformative potential of a confident and proactive attitude towards fear in enhancing human survival and flourishing.

Enhancing self-efficacy to reduce fear

Mastering and enhancing self-efficacy is key in reducing fear and improving one's ability to navigate stressful situations with confidence and composure. By building self-efficacy through practice, positive reinforcement, and acquiring new skills, individuals can increase their belief in their own capabilities to cope with challenges effectively. This proactive approach to self-improvement enables individuals to confront their fears gradually and systematically, ultimately leading to a greater sense of control and mastery over difficult circumstances. Self-efficacy serves as a bridge between instinctual fear responses and rational decision-making, empowering individuals to override primal reactions and act with reason and deliberation. By enhancing self-efficacy, individuals not only strengthen their resilience in the face of fear but also improve their overall quality of life by cultivating a sense of empowerment and self-assurance in challenging situations. Therefore, investing in self-efficacy development is essential for individuals seeking to mitigate the impact of fear on their daily lives and enhance their capacity for survival and success.

Case studies demonstrating increased self-efficacy reducing fear

Throughout various case studies, it has been demonstrated that increased self-efficacy can lead to a reduction in fear responses. By empowering individuals with the belief in their own capabilities to handle challenging situations, fear can be effectively lessened. For example, in studies of individuals with phobias or anxiety disorders, exposure therapy has shown remarkable success in gradually increasing self-efficacy and reducing fear responses. This method involves systematically confronting feared stimuli in a controlled environment, allowing individuals to build confidence in their ability to cope with and overcome their fears. Additionally, case studies of individuals facing life-threatening situations, such as firefighters or soldiers, highlight how training and experience can enhance self-efficacy, leading to a more composed and effective response in the face of danger. Through these cases, it becomes evident that self-efficacy plays a crucial role in managing and diminishing fear, ultimately leading to improved outcomes in high-stress scenarios.

XLVI. Fear and Mindfulness

When considering the intricate relationship between fear and mindfulness, it becomes evident that these two concepts are not necessarily at odds with each other, but rather can work in tandem to enhance human survival. Fear, as a primal instinct deeply rooted in our biology, serves a vital purpose in alerting us to potential threats and dangers. However, it is through mindfulness and conscious awareness that we can learn to manage and harness this fear effectively. Trained individuals, such as soldiers and firefighters, demonstrate how the practice of mindfulness can enable them to remain calm and focused in high-stress situations, ultimately improving their performance under pressure. By repeatedly confronting and gradually overcoming our fears through techniques like exposure therapy and desensitization, we can cultivate a sense of empowerment and resilience. In essence, by mastering our fears through mindfulness, we not only enhance our physical survival but also elevate our quality of life by fostering self-awareness and emotional strength.

Mindfulness practices to manage fear

In the realm of managing fear, mindfulness practices have emerged as a powerful tool to help individuals navigate and overcome challenging situations. By cultivating present-moment awareness and acceptance of one's thoughts and feelings, mindfulness enables individuals to observe fear without necessarily being consumed by it. Research has shown that mindfulness techniques can lead to decreased levels of anxiety and stress, as individuals learn to respond to fear with a sense of calm and clarity. Through regular practice, individuals can develop the ability to recognize when fear arises, acknowledge it, and choose how to respond effectively. By incorporating mindfulness into their daily routine, individuals can gradually rewire their brain's response to fear, ultimately enabling them to confront and manage their fears with greater ease and resilience. In this way, mindfulness practices offer a valuable means of empowering individuals to navigate the complex terrain of fear with greater mastery and confidence.

Benefits of mindfulness in reducing fear responses

The benefits of mindfulness in reducing fear responses are vast and essential for human survival. By practicing mindfulness techniques, individuals can develop a greater sense of self-awareness and emotional regulation, allowing them to respond to fear in a more rational and controlled manner. Mindfulness helps individuals to acknowledge their fear without being overwhelmed by it, enabling them to assess threats accurately and make informed decisions based on reason rather than instinct. Studies have shown that regular mindfulness practice can lead to a decrease in the activation of the amygdala, the part of the brain responsible for processing fear, resulting in a more balanced and less reactive fear response. This ability to remain calm and focused in the face of fear is crucial for overcoming challenges and dangers, ultimately leading to a higher quality of life and improved overall well-being. Therefore, incorporating mindfulness into daily routines can play a significant role in enhancing resilience and reducing the impact of fear on human survival.

Integrating mindfulness into daily routines for fear management

Therefore, integrating mindfulness into daily routines can be a powerful tool for managing fear effectively. By incorporating mindfulness practices such as meditation, deep breathing exercises, and body scans into our regular schedule, we can develop a greater sense of self-awareness and emotional regulation. Mindfulness allows us to observe our thoughts and feelings without judgment, enabling us to identify triggers of fear and anxiety. Through consistent practice, individuals can cultivate the ability to stay present in the moment and respond to fear with a sense of clarity and calmness. This integrative approach can help rewire the brain's response to fear, promoting resilience and emotional well-being. By incorporating mindfulness as a daily habit, we empower ourselves to confront and overcome our fears with a balanced and composed mindset, ultimately enhancing our ability to navigate through challenging situations with confidence and composure.

XLVII. Fear and Lifestyle Changes

Throughout the course of human evolution, fear has played a vital role in guiding our survival instincts. As a natural response to threats, fear triggers our fight-or-flight response, preparing us to confront danger or flee when necessary. However, as society has evolved, fear has taken on new dimensions, influencing lifestyle choices and behaviors. From avoiding certain foods due to health concerns to making career decisions based on anxieties about the future, fear has become a significant factor in shaping our daily routines. While some level of fear is essential for self-preservation, allowing it to dictate our actions can lead to limitations and missed opportunities. By understanding and managing our fears through reason and logic, we can make informed decisions that balance caution with exploration, leading to a more fulfilled and adaptive lifestyle. Ultimately, mastering our fears empowers us to navigate life's challenges with courage and resilience, enhancing both our physical survival and overall well-being.

Lifestyle modifications to reduce fear

Therefore, lifestyle modifications play a crucial role in reducing fear and enhancing overall psychological well-being. Engaging in regular physical exercise, maintaining a healthy diet, and prioritizing adequate sleep can significantly impact emotional regulation and cognitive functioning. Physical activity has been shown to release endorphins, which act as natural mood lifters, while a balanced diet rich in nutrients supports optimal brain function. Moreover, establishing a consistent sleep routine can improve resilience to stress and promote a sense of calm. Additionally, incorporating mindfulness practices and relaxation techniques into daily routines can help individuals better manage their fear responses by fostering a state of inner peace and emotional stability. By making intentional choices to prioritize self-care and mental health, individuals can empower themselves to confront and overcome fears, ultimately leading to a more authentic and fulfilling life.

Role of diet, exercise, and sleep in managing fear

The interplay of diet, exercise, and sleep in managing fear is a crucial aspect of maintaining emotional well-being. A balanced diet rich in nutrients can help regulate mood and reduce anxiety, providing a solid foundation for facing fearful situations. Physical exercise not only promotes overall health but also releases endorphins that can help combat stress and fear. Additionally, regular exercise can improve sleep quality, allowing the body and mind to recover and adapt to daily stressors. Adequate sleep is essential for emotional regulation and resilience, as it allows the brain to process emotions and memories effectively. By prioritizing these three elements in our daily routine, we can better equip ourselves to confront and manage fear in a healthy and proactive manner. In essence, taking care of our bodies through proper nutrition, exercise, and rest can significantly impact our ability to navigate fear and maintain a strong sense of emotional balance.

Long-term benefits of lifestyle changes on fear reduction

It is evident that lifestyle changes can have significant long-term benefits on fear reduction. By incorporating mindfulness practices, regular exercise, and a balanced diet into one's daily routine, individuals can experience a reduction in stress levels and an increased sense of well-being. These lifestyle changes not only have a positive impact on physical health but also on mental health, as they help individuals build resilience and cope with fear in a healthier manner. Over time, these habits can re-wire the brain's response to fear, leading to a decreased sensitivity to perceived threats and a more controlled reaction to stressful situations. Furthermore, the consistency and commitment required to maintain these lifestyle changes can instill a sense of discipline and self-efficacy, further enhancing one's ability to manage fear effectively. Ultimately, embracing a healthy lifestyle can lead to a more balanced and harmonious relationship with fear, promoting overall emotional well-being and quality of life.

XLVIII. Fear and Community Support

Fear and community support go hand in hand in the intricate web of human survival. As individuals, fear can often immobilize us, hinder our decision-making abilities, and leave us feeling isolated. However, within a community, fear can be a unifying force that brings people together to support one another in times of crisis. In the face of danger or uncertainty, communities can provide a sense of security, comfort, and strength that individuals may not find on their own. Whether it be through emotional support, practical assistance, or simply the knowledge that they are not facing their fears alone, communities have the power to bolster individuals' resilience and help them navigate through challenging situations. By fostering a sense of solidarity, trust, and empathy, communities can transform fear from a source of weakness into a source of collective strength, enabling individuals to confront their fears head-on and emerge stronger together.

Importance of community in managing fear

The interplay between fear and community is crucial in effectively managing this primal instinct. While fear is a natural response designed to protect us from harm, it can often be overwhelming when faced alone. This is where the importance of community comes into play – by relying on the support and guidance of others, individuals can gain strength and courage to confront their fears. In times of crisis, communities band together, offering comfort, reassurance, and practical assistance to those in need. Whether it be a natural disaster, a traumatic event, or a personal challenge, the collective power of a community can provide a sense of safety and security that helps individuals overcome their fears. By fostering a sense of belonging and connection, communities create a supportive environment that empowers individuals to face their fears head-on, enabling them to grow and thrive in the face of adversity. Ultimately, the bond of a community can serve as a powerful antidote to fear, offering strength, resilience, and hope in the darkest of times.

Community-based programs to help individuals cope with fear

Recognizing the significant impact fear can have on individuals, community-based programs play a crucial role in helping people cope with their anxieties. By providing a supportive environment where individuals can share their experiences and fears with others, these programs create a sense of solidarity and understanding amongst participants. Through group therapy sessions and workshops, individuals can learn coping mechanisms and strategies to manage their fears effectively. Furthermore, community-based programs often incorporate various mindfulness and relaxation techniques that can help individuals calm their minds and bodies during moments of distress. By offering a safe space for individuals to confront and work through their fears in a supportive and empathetic setting, these programs empower participants to build resilience and develop the tools necessary to navigate challenging situations with confidence and grace. Ultimately, community-based programs serve as a vital resource in fostering emotional well-being and promoting mental health within society.

Success stories of community support reducing fear

Community support has been shown to play a crucial role in reducing fear among individuals. Success stories of communities coming together to provide emotional, physical, and mental assistance during times of crisis have been well documented. For example, in the aftermath of natural disasters, communities mobilize resources to provide shelter, food, and medical aid to those affected, creating a sense of safety and security. By offering a supportive network, individuals are able to lean on each other for strength and reassurance, ultimately reducing their feelings of fear and vulnerability. This sense of solidarity and unity instills a belief in individuals that they are not alone in facing their challenges, fostering resilience and a sense of empowerment. Additionally, community support can also provide opportunities for individuals to share their experiences, fears, and anxieties, creating a collective understanding and empathy that diminishes the isolating effects of fear. Ultimately, success stories of community support showcase the transformative power of human connection in alleviating fear and promoting emotional well-being.

XLIX. Fear and Technology Solutions

Throughout history, fear has been a driving force behind human survival instincts, triggering our fight or flight responses in the face of danger. However, as society evolves and technology advances, new solutions are emerging to address and manage our innate fears. Modern advancements in technology, such as virtual reality exposure therapy, biofeedback techniques, and AI-driven cognitive behavioral therapy apps, provide innovative tools for individuals to confront and overcome their fears in a controlled environment. By combining these technological solutions with traditional psychological practices, individuals can learn to rewire their brain's fear responses and develop coping strategies for navigating anxiety-inducing situations. This integration of fear and technology solutions represents a new frontier in the field of mental health and personal development, offering individuals the opportunity to harness the power of fear as a catalyst for growth and self-improvement.

Technological innovations to help manage fear

The evolution of fear as a natural response to survival has led to the development of technological innovations aimed at helping individuals manage this instinct in modern times. As our understanding of the human brain and behavior continues to advance, new tools and techniques have emerged to assist in controlling fear responses. For instance, virtual reality exposure therapy has been shown to be effective in treating phobias and anxiety disorders by providing a safe and controlled environment for individuals to confront their fears. Additionally, biofeedback devices can help individuals monitor their physiological responses to fear and learn to regulate them through techniques such as deep breathing and mindfulness. These technological advancements offer new ways for individuals to confront and overcome their fears, ultimately empowering them to navigate high-stress situations with greater composure and resilience. By combining scientific knowledge with innovative tools, we can harness the power of technology to master our primal instincts and thrive in the face of fear.

Virtual reality and AI in fear reduction therapies

Throughout history, fear has been an intrinsic part of human survival, serving as a protective mechanism to alert us to potential threats in our environment. However, as our understanding of the human psyche evolves, so do the methods by which we can effectively manage and overcome our fears. Virtual reality and artificial intelligence have emerged as promising tools in fear reduction therapies, offering a safe and controlled environment in which individuals can confront their fears gradually. By immersing patients in simulated scenarios that trigger their anxieties, therapists can guide them through exposure therapy in a controlled setting, allowing for desensitization without the risks associated with real-life exposure. Furthermore, AI can personalize these experiences based on individual responses, enhancing the efficacy of the treatment. By incorporating virtual reality and AI into fear reduction therapies, we can revolutionize the way we approach and conquer our fears, ultimately improving our quality of life and mental well-being.

Future potential of technology in fear management

Further advancements in technology offer a promising future for fear management. Virtual reality simulations, for example, provide a controlled environment in which individuals can gradually confront and overcome their fears through exposure therapy. These simulations can tailor the intensity of the experience to the individual's comfort level, allowing for a personalized approach to fear management. Additionally, wearable devices that monitor physiological responses to stress can help individuals recognize early signs of fear and implement coping strategies before it escalates. The integration of artificial intelligence in these devices could provide real-time feedback and guidance to help individuals better manage their fear responses. Overall, utilizing technology in fear management not only enhances the effectiveness of traditional techniques but also opens up new avenues for personalized and innovative approaches to overcoming fear. As technology continues to advance, the potential for more sophisticated and effective fear management tools will only increase, ultimately empowering individuals to confront and conquer their fears with confidence and resilience.

L. Fear and Future Prospects

Throughout history, fear has been a driving force behind human behavior, serving as a powerful instinct for survival. As we navigate the complexities of the modern world, our relationship with fear has become increasingly nuanced, requiring a balance between instinct and reason. Future prospects for humanity rest on our ability to harness and control our fears, utilizing advancements in technology and psychology to empower ourselves in the face of uncertainty. By understanding the evolutionary roots of our fears and implementing strategies for managing them, we can navigate challenging situations with a sense of calm and clarity. Through deliberate practice and exposure to our fears, we can gradually desensitize ourselves and cultivate resilience in the face of adversity. Ultimately, mastering our fears not only enhances our physical survival but also enriches our quality of life, enabling us to embrace fear as a valuable ally in our journey towards self-awareness and personal growth.

Emerging trends in understanding and managing fear

Having established fear as a natural response crucial for survival, the evolving trends in understanding and managing fear are becoming more nuanced. In today's world, where threats can be psychological as well as physical, the ability to control fear is gaining recognition as a critical skill. Trained professionals in high-risk fields demonstrate the effectiveness of managing fear through a combination of psychological techniques and physical training. By exposing oneself gradually to fears and desensitizing the body and mind, individuals can improve their ability to maintain composure in stressful situations. This shift in perception towards fear as a manageable emotion rather than an overwhelming force emphasizes the importance of self-awareness and resilience. As our understanding of fear expands, so does our capacity to navigate the complexities of modern life with courage and clarity. Mastering fear not only enhances survival instincts but also enriches the quality of our daily experiences.

Potential future challenges in fear management

Throughout history, the ability to manage fear has been crucial in ensuring human survival. However, as we progress into the future, new challenges may arise that test our capacity to navigate the complexities of fear. One potential challenge is the rapid advancement of technology, which exposes us to a constant influx of information that can trigger anxiety and fear. With social media platforms constantly bombarding us with news of global crises and personal emergencies, it can be challenging to discern legitimate threats from exaggerated ones. Furthermore, as artificial intelligence continues to evolve, the fear of job displacement and loss of privacy may become more prevalent. Another future challenge in fear management could stem from environmental factors such as climate change, which has the potential to heighten existential fears about the future of our planet. As we move forward, it will be essential to develop new strategies and techniques to effectively manage fear in the face of these emerging challenges.

Vision for a society better equipped to handle fear

In envisioning a society better equipped to handle fear, it is crucial to emphasize the cultivation of emotional intelligence alongside technological advancements. By promoting a culture that values introspection and self-awareness, individuals can develop the mental resilience needed to confront their fears with a calm and rational mindset. This can be achieved through education and mindfulness practices that teach individuals how to acknowledge and process their emotions effectively. Additionally, investing in mental health resources and support systems can provide people with the tools they need to navigate through challenging situations and emerge stronger. By fostering a community that prioritizes emotional well-being and equips its members with the necessary skills to manage fear, we can create a society that thrives in the face of adversity and demonstrates the power of human resilience. The integration of emotional intelligence with technological innovations can lead to a future where fear is not seen as a barrier, but as a catalyst for personal growth and collective strength.

LI. Conclusion

In conclusion, the intricate interplay between fear and human survival is a delicate balance that has evolved over millennia. While fear is a primal instinct crucial for detecting and responding to threats, it must be tempered by reason and modern techniques to ensure optimal outcomes in high-stakes environments. By examining how trained professionals like firefighters and soldiers harness their fear to perform under pressure, we see that fear can be mastered and managed through practice and discipline. Moreover, the notion of repeatedly confronting fears to overcome them demonstrates the importance of gradual exposure and systematic desensitization in building resilience. Ultimately, the ability to control fear not only enhances physical survival but also contributes to a higher quality of life. By viewing fear as a potent ally rather than a formidable foe, individuals can tap into their inner strength and fortitude, leading to greater self-awareness and psychological well-being.

Summary of key points discussed

Throughout this essay, the discussion has revolved around the intricate interplay between fear and human survival. It has been underscored that fear, as a primal instinct, is deeply ingrained in our biology as a critical response mechanism to threats. Moreover, the text delves into the idea of mastering fear, emphasizing the importance of controlling it in high-stress situations for optimal performance. Techniques to manage fear, both psychologically and physically, have been explored, highlighting how individuals can develop the skill of remaining calm and focused under pressure. Another key point that has emerged is the necessity of confronting fears repeatedly in order to overcome them, with strategies like gradual exposure and desensitization being effective tools in this process. Ultimately, the essay argues that by understanding and managing fear effectively, individuals can not only enhance their chances of physical survival but also significantly improve their overall quality of life. Fear, therefore, is portrayed not as an adversary but as a valuable ally that can lead to greater self-awareness and resilience when properly harnessed.

Reflection on the dual nature of fear as both a protective and limiting factor

Throughout the course of human history, fear has served as a double-edged sword, both protecting us from danger and constraining our actions. At its core, fear is a primal instinct that has evolved to ensure our survival in the face of threats. This instinctual response triggers a cascade of physiological reactions that prepare us to fight or flee. However, in the modern world, where many threats are not immediate or life-threatening, fear can become a limiting factor, holding us back from taking risks or pursuing our goals. While fear may be a necessary survival mechanism, it is crucial to recognize when it is inhibiting our growth and development. By acknowledging and understanding our fears, we can begin to confront them and work towards overcoming their grip on our lives. Through a combination of reason, practice, and self-awareness, we can learn to harness the protective aspects of fear while minimizing its limiting effects, ultimately leading to a more fulfilled and resilient existence.

Final thoughts on mastering fear for enhanced survival and quality of life

In mastering fear for enhanced survival and quality of life, it is imperative to acknowledge fear as a natural response rooted in our evolutionary history. However, the essence lies in controlling and leveraging this instinct for our benefit. Through training and exposure, individuals can learn to confront and manage their fears effectively, allowing them to perform optimally in high-pressure situations. By adopting psychological and physical techniques, individuals can cultivate the ability to remain calm and clear-headed, even amidst adversity. This mastery of fear not only enhances physical survival but also contributes to an improved quality of life. Viewing fear as a potential ally rather than an enemy can lead to increased self-awareness and resilience, empowering individuals to navigate challenging circumstances with composure and confidence. Thus, by embracing fear as a tool for personal growth and development, individuals can unlock new levels of potential and thrive in the face of uncertainty.

Bibliography

David Lindner. 'Mastering Public Speaking - How to Deal with Fear of Public Speaking.' Dr. Patrick Johnson, 2/7/2023

Harald Tauchmann. 'The Causal Impact of Fear of Unemployment on Psychological Health.' Arndt R. Reichert, RUB, Department of Economics, 1/1/2011

Pui-lam Law. 'New Connectivities in China.' Virtual, Actual and Local Interactions, Springer Science & Business Media, 3/30/2012

Lytras, Miltiadis D.. 'Emerging Topics and Technologies in Information Systems.' IGI Global, 2/28/2009

Constantin Cranganu. 'Reflecting on our Changing Climate, from Fear to Facts.' A Voice in the Wilderness, Cambridge Scholars Publishing, 3/7/2024

Jerry J. Buccafusco. 'Methods of Behavior Analysis in Neuroscience.' CRC Press, 8/29/2000

Dan Gardner. 'Risk.' The Science and Politics of Fear, McClelland & Stewart, 2/24/2009

Gurukul. 'Chapterwise Objective MCQs Science (PCB) Book for CBSE Class 12 Term I Exam.' Gurukul Books & Packaging, 8/23/2021

Yongjian Bao. 'Affect and cognition in upper echelons' strategic decision making: Empirical and theoretical studies for advancing corporate governance..' Matteo Cristofaro, Frontiers Media SA, 2/15/2023

Charles B. Guignon. 'The Existentialists.' Critical Essays on Kierkegaard, Nietzsche, Heidegger, and Sartre, Rowman & Littlefield Publishers, 10/26/2004

Sergio Starkstein. 'A Conceptual and Therapeutic Analysis of Fear.' Springer, 4/17/2018

Donald Rutherford. 'Oxford Studies in Early Modern Philosophy, Volume XI.' Oxford University Press, 10/20/2022

Ted Orland. 'Art & Fear.' Observations on the Perils (and Rewards) of Artmaking, David Bayles, Souvenir Press, 2/9/2023

Mingwei Song. 'Fear of Seeing.' A Poetics of Chinese Science Fiction, Columbia University Press, 10/3/2023

Dominic Ingemark. 'Representations of Fear.' Verbalising Emotion in Ancient Roman Folk Narrative, Camilla Asplund Ingemark, Tallinn Book Printers, 1/1/2020

Kristen Ulmer. 'The Art of Fear.' Why Conquering Fear Won't Work and What to Do Instead, HarperCollins, 6/13/2017

Charles R. Cooper. 'The St. Martin's Guide to Writing.' Rise B. Axelrod, Macmillan, 1/26/2010

Jason C Bivins. 'Religion of Fear.' The Politics of Horror in Conservative Evangelicalism, Oxford University Press, 8/29/2008

Michael Kinnamon. 'The Witness of Religion in an Age of Fear.' Westminster John Knox Press, 3/10/2017

Elemér Hankiss. 'Fears and Symbols.' An Introduction to the Study of Western Civilization, Central European University Press, 1/1/2001

j.c davis. 'Fear,myth & History.' cambridge univ.Press, 1/1/1986

Lee T Copping. 'Sex Differences in Fear Response.' An Evolutionary Perspective, Anne Campbell, Springer Nature, 4/10/2021

R. Michael Fisher. 'The Fear Problematique.' Role of Philosophy of Education in Speaking Truths to Powers in a Culture of Fear, IAP, 11/1/2023

Christopher Campbell. 'The Routledge Companion to Media and Race.' Routledge, 11/3/2016

Teri Smith-Pickens. 'The Irrational Fear Cure.' In Four Miraculous Steps, Independently Published, 6/2/2021

Srinivasan S. Pillay, M.D.. 'Life Unlocked.' 7 Revolutionary Lessons to Overcome Fear, Harmony/Rodale, 8/30/2011

Julie Davis. 'No More Monsters in the Closet.' Teaching Your Children to Overcome Everyday Fears and Phobias, Jeffrey L. Brown, Prince Paperbacks, 1/1/1995

Lorna Garano. 'Coping with Anxiety.' Ten Simple Ways to Relieve Anxiety, Fear, and Worry, Edmund J. Bourne, New Harbinger Publications, 4/1/2016

Educational Testing Service. 'The Origins of Fear.' Wiley, 1/1/1974

Peter Muris. 'Normal and Abnormal Fear and Anxiety in Children and Adolescents.' Elsevier, 7/7/2010

Joseph LeDoux. 'Anxious.' Using the Brain to Understand and Treat Fear and Anxiety, Penguin, 8/23/2016

Patrick Kimuyu. 'The Role of Behavioral and Cognitive Theory in Phobia Development and Extinction.' GRIN Verlag, 4/11/2018

Paul L. Gower. 'Psychology of Fear.' Nova Science Publishers, 1/1/2004

Educational Foundation for Nuclear Science, Inc.. 'Bulletin of the Atomic Scientists.' Educational Foundation for Nuclear Science, Inc., 6/1/1970

National Collaborating Centre for Mental Health (Great Britain). 'Social Anxiety Disorder.' Recognition, Assessment and Treatment, Royal College of Psychiatrists, 1/1/2013

Patrick Fanning. 'Mind and Emotions.' A Universal Treatment for Emotional Disorders, Matthew McKay, New Harbinger Publications, 7/1/2011

W. Sluckin. 'Fear in Animals and Man.' Van Nostrand Reinhold Company, 1/1/1979

Ronald Hutton. 'The Witch.' A History of Fear, from Ancient Times to the Present, Yale University Press, 1/1/2017

Jason C. Whitehead. 'Redeeming Fear.' A Constructive Theology for Living Into Hope, Fortress Press, 6/1/2013

Ahmed Bayouda. 'Endocrine System.' The Secrets of Hormonal Balance, Ahmed Bayouda, 4/1/2024

Akira Arimura. 'Pituitary Adenylate Cyclase-Activating Polypeptide.' Hubert Vaudry, Springer Science & Business Media, 12/6/2012

Terrence Keane. 'Post-Traumatic Stress Disorder.' Basic Science and Clinical Practice, Peter Shiromani, Springer Science & Business Media, 3/6/2009

Elizabeth A. Phelps. 'The Human Amygdala.' Paul J. Whalen, Guilford Press, 1/1/2009

Institute of Medicine. 'Transforming the Workforce for Children Birth Through Age 8.' A Unifying Foundation, National Research Council, National Academies Press, 7/23/2015

Daniel T. Blumstein. 'The Nature of Fear.' Harvard University Press, 9/8/2020

B.G. Konopelchenko. 'Introduction to Multidimensional Integrable Equations.' The Inverse Spectral Transform in 2+1 Dimensions, Springer Science & Business Media, 6/29/2013